CHRISTIANS AND ECONOMICS
A Biblical Point of View

KERBY ANDERSON

For the love of money is a root of all sorts of evil.—1 Tim. 6:10, NASB.

CHRISTIANS AND ECONOMICS

A Biblical Point of View

Kerby Anderson

Christian Publishing House
Cambridge, Ohio

Copyright © 2016 Kerby Anderson

All rights reserved. Except for brief quotations in articles, other publications, book reviews, and blogs, no part of this book may be reproduced in any manner without prior written permission from the publishers. For information, write,

support@christianpublishers.org

Unless otherwise stated, Scripture quotations are from *New American Standard Bible (NASB)* Copyright © 1960, 1962, 1963, 1968, 1971, 1972, 1973, 1975, 1977, **1995** by The Lockman Foundation

CHRISTIANS AND ECONOMICS A Biblical Point of View by Kerby Anderson

ISBN-13: 978-1-945757-04-4

ISBN-10: 1-945757-04-3

Table of Contents

Preface 2
SECTION 1 Christian Principles 3
   CHAPTER 1 Bible and Economics 4
      Biblical View of Human Nature 5
      Biblical View of Private Property 7
      Biblical View of Work 8
      Role of Government 11
      Free Enterprise System 13
      Economic Criticisms of Capitalism 14
      Moral Criticisms of Capitalism 16
   CHAPTER 2 Ethics and Economics 18
      Biblical View of Private Property 19
      Biblical View of Work 20
      Biblical View of Government 22
      Conclusion 24
SECTION 2 Economic Systems 26
   CHAPTER 3 Capitalism and Socialism 27
      The War Over Capitalism 28
      Economic Criticisms 30
      Moral Criticism 31
      The Zero-Sum Myth 33
   CHAPTER 4 Hayek and the Road to Serfdom... 35
   CHAPTER 5 Misconceptions About The Road to Serfdom 37

Paved With Good Intentions..........................40

Biblical Perspective 43

CHAPTER 6 Wealth and Poverty.......................45

A Biblical View of Wealth 45

A Biblical View of Poverty 47

Poverty and Government 48

Poverty and the Church 49

Breaking the Cycle of Poverty 50

The Christian Lifestyle 52

CHAPTER 7 Debt and Credit 55

The Consequences of Debt.............................56

Credit Card Debt 58

Home Mortgage..59

Getting Out of Debt 61

SECTION 3 Challenges in the 21st Century 63

CHAPTER 8 Is the World Flat? 64

The Flatteners..65

Biblical Perspective 71

CHAPTER 9 Globalization and the Wal-Mart Effect...73

The Wal-Mart Effect 74

Out of the Box 76

Salmon 78

Consumer Behavior 80

CHAPTER 10 Is America Broke? 82

Fannie Mae and Freddie Mac.........................83

Medicare 85
Consumer Debt 87
Biblical Perspective 88
CHAPTER 11 Do We Have Financial Security? ... 90
Savings 91
Corporate Pensions 93
Social Security 94
Retirement 96
CHAPTER 12 Economics: Past and Future 99
The Bailout 99
What Caused the Financial Crisis? 101
The End of Prosperity 102
The Future of Affluence 104
Squanderville 106
CHAPTER 13 Consumerism and Materialism 109
Inverted Values and Changing Attitudes 111
Undermining the Family and Church 113
Undermining the Community and Character .115
A Biblical Perspective on Materialism and Consumerism 116
APPENDIX Bible Verses on Economics and Finance 119

Bibliography 120

Other Books by Kerby Anderson 121

vii

Kerby Anderson

Kerby Anderson is the President of Probe Ministries. He holds masters degrees from Yale University (science) and Georgetown University (government).

He also serves as a visiting professor at Dallas Theological Seminary and has spoken on dozens of university campuses including University of Michigan, Vanderbilt University, Princeton University, Johns Hopkins University, University of Colorado and University of Texas.

He is the author of fifteen books including *Signs of Warning, Signs of Hope*, *Moral Dilemmas*, *Christian Ethics in Plain Language*, *A Biblical Point of View on Islam*, *A Biblical Point of View on Homosexuality*, *A Biblical Point of View on Intelligent Design*, *A Biblical Point of View on Spiritual Warfare*, and *Managing Your Money in Tough Times*. He is also the editor of many books including *Marriage, Family, & Sexuality* and *Technology, Spirituality, & Social Trends*.

He is the host of "Point of View" radio talk show and regular guest on "Fire Away" (American Family Radio). He has appeared or numerous radio and TV talk shows including the "MacNeil/Lehrer News Hour," "Focus on the Family," "Beverly LaHaye Live," and "The 700 Club."

He produces a daily syndicated radio commentary and writes editorials that have appeared in the *Dallas Morning News*, the *Miami Herald*, the *San Jose Mercury*, and the *Houston Post*. His radio commentaries have been syndicated by International Media Services, United Press International, American Family Radio, Moody Radio, and the USA Radio Network.

Kerby is married to Susanne and is the father of three grown children.

Preface

How should Christians think about economic issues? We live in a world affected by economic trends and economic policies. What does the Bible say about economics? How should Christians think about work, wealth, and poverty? How should we react to globalization and a world economy?

These are some of the important issues that we consider in this book. The chapters in this originally aired as Probe Ministries radio programs and have been edited into chapters that address various aspects economics, finance, and business. Because they aired in different years, there is occasionally some overlap of content. This is helpful since we often look at a different aspect of the same issue, and repetition is a helpful aid in learning.

The first section sets forth the biblical principles about economics. The second section addresses the subject of economic systems (capitalism, socialism) and economic issues that surface as we discuss these economic systems.

The third section deals with the many challenges we face in the 21st century. These range from globalization and the flat world to the finances challenges we face as a nation from debt and governmental entitlements. It also provides practical suggestions about how to avoid materialism and how to live in a world of consumerism.

The Bible admonishes us to be good stewards (work heartily as for the Lord – Colossians 3:23) and to keep our life free from the love of money (Hebrews 13:5) so that we will be content with what we have. The Bible reminds us that, "the love of money is a root of all kinds of evils" (1 Timothy 6:10). May we learn to use money wisely and live godly lives.

SECTION 1 Christian Principles

CHAPTER 1 Bible and Economics

How are we to develop a Christian view of economics? The Bible provides a firm moral foundation for economics, but that is not how economics is taught today. A few centuries ago, there was much greater emphasis given to the moral aspect of economics.

For examples, if you look at the *Summa Theologica* written by Thomas Aquinas, you find whole sections of his theological work devoted to economic issues. He asked such questions as, "What is a just price?" or "How should we deal with poverty?"

Today, these questions, if they are even discussed at all, would be discussed in a class on economic theory. But in his time, these were theological questions that were a critical and integral part of the educational curricula.

In the Protestant Reformation, we find the same thing. In John Calvin's *Institutes of the Christian Religion*, whole sections are devoted to government and economics. Therefore, Christians should not feel that economics is outside the domain of Christian thinking. If anything, we need to recapture this arena and bring a strong biblical message to it.

As we have already seen in the book, the Bible speaks to economic issues more than any other issue. Whole sections of the book of Proverbs and many of the parables of Jesus deal with economic matters. They tell us what our attitude should be toward wealth and how a Christian should handle his or her finances. The Bible also provides a description of human nature, which helps us evaluate the possible success of an economic system in society.

Biblical View of Human Nature

The Bible teaches that there are two aspects to human nature. First, we are created in the image of God and thus able to control the economic system. But second, human beings are sinful and thus tend towards greed and exploitation. This points to the need to protect individuals from human sinfulness in the economic system. Therefore, Christians have a much more balanced view of economics and can, therefore, construct economic theories and analyze existing economic systems.

Christians should see the fallacy of such utopian economic theories because they fail to take seriously human sinfulness. Instead of changing people from the inside out as the gospel does, Marxists believe that people will be changed from the outside in. Change the economic base, they say, and you will change human beings. This is one of the reasons that Marxism was doomed to failure because it did not take into account human sinfulness and our need for spiritual redemption.

When we are looking at either theories of government or theories of economics, an important starting point is our view of human nature. This helps us analyze these theories and predict their possible success in society. Therefore, we must go to the Scriptures to evaluate the very foundation of each economic theory.

First, the Bible says that human beings are created in the image of God. This implies that we have rationality and responsibility. Because we have rationality and volition, we can choose between various competing products and services. Furthermore, we can function within a market system in which people can exercise their power of choice. We are not like the animals that are governed by instinct. We are governed by rationality and can make meaningful choices within a market system.

We can also assume that private property can exist within this system because of the biblical idea of dominion. In Genesis 1:28, God says we are to subdue the earth and have dominion over the creation. Certainly, one aspect of this is that humans can own property in which they can exercise their dominion.

Since we have both volition and private property rights, we can then assume that we should have the freedom to exchange these private property rights in a free market where goods and services can be exchanged.

The second part of human nature is also important. The Bible describes the fall of the world and the fall of mankind. We are fallen creatures with a sin nature. This sinfulness manifests itself in selfishness, greed, and exploitation. Thus, we need some protection in an economic system from the sinful effects of human interaction.

Since the Bible teaches about the effects of sinful behavior on the world, we should be concerned about any system that would concentrate economic power and thereby unleash the ravages of sinful behavior on the society. Christians, therefore, should reject state-controlled or centrally controlled economies, which would concentrate power in the hands of a few sinful individuals. Instead, we should support an economic system that would disperse that power and protect us from greed and exploitation.

Finally, we should also recognize that not only is human nature fallen, but the world is fallen. The world has become a place of decay and scarcity. In a fallen world, we have to be good managers of the limited resources that can be made available in a market economy. God has given us dominion over His creation, and we must be good stewards of the resources at our disposal.

Biblical View of Private Property

The Bible provides some general principles related to property. First, the Bible clearly teaches that everything in the world belongs to the Lord. Psalm 24:1 says, "The earth is the Lord's, and all it contains, the world, and those who dwell in it."

At the same time, the Bible also teaches that we are given dominion over the creation (Genesis 1:28). We are accountable to God for our stewardship of the resources. Because God owns it all (Psalm 24:1), no one owns property in perpetuity. But the Bible does grants private property rights to individuals. One of the Ten Commandments prohibits stealing, thus approving of private property rights. The book of Exodus establishes the rights of property owners and the liabilities of those who violate those rights. Financial restitution (Exodus 22) must be made to property owners in cases of theft or neglect. Physical force is allowed to protect property (Exodus 22:2). Lost animals are to be returned, even when they belong to an enemy (Exodus 23:4). Removing landmarks that protect property is clearly forbidden (Deuteronomy 19:14; 27:17; Job 24:2; Proverbs 22:28; Hosea 5:10).

Some Christians have suggested that the New Testament rejects the idea of private property because the book of Acts teaches that the early Christians held property in common. But this communal sharing in the New Testament was voluntary. Acts 2:44-47 says: "And all those who had believed were together and had all things in common; and they began selling their property and possessions and were sharing them with all, as anyone might have need. Day by day continuing with one mind in the temple, and breaking bread from house to house; they were taking their meals together with gladness and sincerity of heart, praising God and having favor with all the people. And the Lord was adding to their number day by day those who were being saved."

The early Christians did not reject the idea of private property. Notice that they still retained private property rights until they voluntarily gave up those rights to help other believers in Jerusalem. This was a specific leading of the Holy Spirit to meet the increasing needs of the growing New Testament church.

We can see that they retained property rights in the actions of Ananias and Sapphira. Their sin was not that they retained control of some of their property but that they lied about it. Acts 5:4: "While it remained unsold, did it not remain your own? And after it was sold, was it not under your control? Why is it that you have conceived this deed in your heart? You have not lied to men but to God."

Also notice that Paul called for voluntary charity toward believers in Jerusalem when he called New Testament believers to give to the needs of those within the church. 2 Corinthians 8:13-15 says, "For this is not for the ease of others and for your affliction, but by way of equality—at this present time your abundance being a supply for their need, so that their abundance also may become a supply for your need, that there may be equality; as it is written, 'He who gathered much did not have too much, and he who gathered little had no lack.'"

Biblical View of Work

What is the place of work in economic activity? We should begin by clearing up a major misconception. Many Christians think that we work because of the fall (Genesis 3). Actually, that is not true. Work is not a product of the fall but is actually part of the creation order (Genesis 2:15-17). While it is true that work was deformed by the fall so that there is now toil and drudgery.

God created us to work the land and be productive. Through work, we are given the opportunity to design and create. Because of Christ's redemptive work on our behalf, all of us can be involved in meaningful work that is good and reflects His redemptive purpose.

Second, we are created in God's image (Genesis 1:27), so we can find work rewarding and empowering. We are given the privilege by God of enjoying the earth and deriving profit and benefit from what it might produce (Genesis 9:1-3). At the same time, we should also be held accountable for the work we do or fail to do. When Paul wrote to the Thessalonians, he devoted a portion of his epistles to the importance of work for the Christian. In 1 Thessalonians 4:11-12 he said: "Make it your ambition to lead a quiet life and attend to your own business and work with your hands, just as we commanded you so that you will behave properly toward outsiders and not be in any need." He also warns in 2 Thessalonians 3:10 that "if anyone is not willing to work, then he is not to eat, either."

Third, there is also a satisfaction in work. It not only satisfies a basic human need but it also is a privilege provided by the hand of God. Ecclesiastes 2:24 says, "There is nothing better for a man than to eat and drink and tell himself that his labor is good. This also I have seen that it is from the hand of God."

The Proverbs talk about the importance and benefits of work. Proverbs 12:11 says: "He who tills his land will have plenty of bread, But he who pursues worthless things lacks sense." Proverbs 13:4 says: "The soul of the sluggard craves and gets nothing, But the soul of the diligent is made fat." And Proverbs 14:23 says, "In all labor there is profit, But mere talk leads only to poverty."

Fourth, we are to work unto the Lord. Paul admonishes believers to "work heartily as for the Lord rather than for men" (Colossians 3:23). Paul also says in 1 Corinthians 1:26-31:

> For consider your calling, brethren, that there were not many wise according to the flesh, not many mighty, not many noble; but God has chosen the foolish things of the world to shame the wise, and God has chosen the weak things of the world to shame the things which are strong, and the base things of the world and the despised God has chosen, the things that are not, so that He may nullify the things that are, so that no man may boast before God. But by His doing you are in Christ Jesus, who became to us wisdom from God, and righteousness and sanctification, and redemption, so that, just as it is written, "Let him who boasts, boast in the Lord."

We also learn from Scripture that without God's involvement in our work, human labor is futile. Psalm 127:1 says, "Unless the Lord builds the house, they labor in vain who build it." God's blessings come to us through our labors.

Finally, with work there should also be rest. The law of the Sabbath (Ex. 20:8-11) and the other Old Testament provisions for feasts and rest demonstrate the importance of rest. In the New Testament also we see that Jesus set a pattern for rest (Mark 6:45-47; Luke 6:12) in His ministry. Believers are to work for the Lord and His Kingdom, but they must also avoid being workaholics and take the time to rest.

We should also mention the opposite of work. The Bible warns us of the consequences of idleness. Proverbs 24:30-34 says,

I passed by the field of the sluggard and by the vineyard of the man lacking sense, and behold, it was completely overgrown with thistles; Its surface was covered with nettles and its stone wall was broken down. When I saw, I reflected upon it; I looked, and received instruction. A little sleep, a little slumber, A little folding of the hands to rest, Then your poverty will come as a robber and your want like an armed man.

Role of Government

The Bible gives some clear principles concerning government. First, Christians are commanded to obey government (Romans 13:1) and submit to civil authority (1 Peter 2:13–17). We are called to render service and obedience to the government (Matthew 22:21). However, we are not to render total submission. There may be a time in which Christians may be called to disobey government leaders who have set themselves in opposition to divine law (Romans 13:1-5; John 19:11). We are to obey civil authorities (Romans13:5) in order to avoid anarchy and chaos, but there may be times when we may be forced to obey God rather than men (Acts 5:29).

Second, we understand that because of the fall (Genesis 3), all have a sin nature (Romans 3:23). Government must, therefore, administer justice in the political and economic realm. It must also protect us against aggression as well as provide for public works (1 Kings 10:9).

The reality of sin nature dictates that we not allow a political concentration of power. Governmental power should be limited to appropriate checks and balances. Government also should not be used in a coercive way to attempt to change individuals. We should not accept the idea that the state can transform people from the outside. Only the gospel can change people from the inside and so that they become new creatures (2 Corinthians 5:17).

Consider these four functions of government in the economic realm. Government must ensure justice in the following ways:

• "Weights and scales are to be honest, a full measure (shaken down) is to be given (Leviticus 19:35-36; Deuteronomy 25:15; Prov. 20:23; Luke 6:38), and currency is not be debased by inflationary monetary policy or other means (e.g., mixing lead with silver)."

• Procedural justice requires that contracts and commitments be honored (Leviticus 19:13).

• Government must also ensure justice when people are cheated or swindled. In these cases, the cost of restoration should be borne by the guilty or negligent party (Exodus 21:33-36; 22:5-8, 10-15). Government should also deal with those who give a false accusation (Deuteronomy 19:16-19).

• Government should also prevent economic discrimination. This would apply to those of different economic class (James 2:1-4) as well as to those of different sex, race, and religious background (Galatians 3:26-29). Government can exert a great influence on the economy and therefore should use its regulatory power to protect against discrimination.

That being said, the primary function of government is to set the rules and provide a means of redress. The free market should be allowed to function with government providing the necessary economic boundaries and protections. Once this is done in the free enterprise system, individuals are free to use their economic choices in a free market.

Free Enterprise System

The philosophical foundation for capitalism can be found in the publication of *The Wealth of Nations*, written by Adam Smith in 1776. He argued that the mercantile economic system working at that time in Great Britain was not the best economic foundation. Instead, he argued that the wealth of nations could be increased by allowing the individual to seek his own self-interest and by removing governmental control over the economy.

His theory rested on three major premises. First, his system was based on the observation that people are motivated by self-interest. He said, "It is not from the benevolence of the butcher, the brewer, or the baker that we expect our dinner, but from their regard to their own interest." Smith went on to say that "neither intends to promote the public interest," yet each is "led by an invisible hand to promote an end that was not part of [his] intention."[1]

A second premise of Adam Smith was the acceptance of private property. Property was not to be held in common but owned and freely traded in a market system. Profits generated from the use and exchange of private property rights provided incentive and became the mechanism that drives the capitalist system.

From a Christian perspective, we can see that the basis of private property rests in our being created in God's image. We can make choices over property that we can exchange in a market system. The need for private property grows out of our sinfulness. Our sinful nature produces laziness, neglect, and slothfulness.

---

[1] Adam Smith, *The Wealth of Nations*, Book 4, Chapter 2 (1776).

Economic justice can best be achieved if each person is accountable for his own productivity.

The third premise of Adam Smith's theory was the minimization of the role of government. Borrowing a phrase from the French physiocrats, he called this laissez-faire. Smith argued that we should decrease the role of government and increase the role of a free market.

Historically, capitalism has had a number of advantages. It has liberated economic potential. It has also provided the foundation for a great deal of political and economic freedom. When government is not controlling markets, then there is economic freedom to be involved in a whole array of entrepreneurial activities.

Capitalism has also led to a great deal of political freedom, because once you limit the role of government in economics, you limit the scope of government in other areas. It is no accident that most of the countries with the greatest political freedom usually have a great deal of economic freedom.

This does not mean that Christians should endorse every aspect of capitalism. For example, many proponents of capitalism hold a view known as utilitarianism, which is opposed to the notion of biblical absolutes. Certainly, we must reject this philosophy as well as some of the abuses of capitalism.

Economic Criticisms of Capitalism

The first economic criticism is that capitalism leads to monopolies. These develop for two reasons: too little government and too much government. Monopolies have occurred in the past because government has not been willing to exercise its God-given authority. Government finally stepped in and broke up the big trusts that were not allowing the free enterprise system to function correctly.

But in recent decades, the reason for monopolies has often been too much government. Many of the largest monopolies today are government sanctioned or sponsored monopolies that prevent true competition from taking place. The solution is for government to allow a freer market where competition can take place.

Let me add that many people often call markets with limited competition monopolies when the term is not appropriate. For example, the major car companies may seem like a monopoly or oligopoly until you realize that in the market of consumer durables the true market is the entire western world.

The second criticism of capitalism is that it leads to pollution. In a capitalistic system, pollutants are considered externalities. The producer will incur costs that are external to the firm so often there is no incentive to clean up the pollution. Instead, it is dumped into areas held in common such as the air or water.

The solution, in this case, is governmental regulation. However, this need not be a justification for building a massive bureaucracy. We need to find creative ways to direct self-interest so that people work towards the common good.

Sometimes when speaking on the topic of government and the environment, I use a thought experiment. Most communities use the water supply from a river and dump treated waste back into the water to flow downstream. Often there is a tendency to cut corners and leave the waste treatment problem for those downstream. But imagine if you required that the water intake pipe is downstream, and the waste pipe is upstream. If you did require this (and this is only a thought experiment), you would instantly guarantee that you would have less of a problem with water pollution. Why? It is now in the self-interest of the community to clean the wastewater being pumped back into the river. So while there is a need for governmental action, much less might be needed if we think of creative ways to constrain self-interest and make it work for the common good.

We can acknowledge that although there are some valid economic criticisms of capitalism, these can be controlled by limited governmental control. And when capitalism is wisely controlled, it generates significant economic prosperity and economic freedom for its citizens.

Moral Criticisms of Capitalism

One of the moral arguments against capitalism involves the issue of greed. And this is why many Christians feel ambivalent towards the free enterprise system. After all, some critics of capitalism contend that this economic system makes people greedy.

To answer this question, we need to resolve the following question. Does capitalism make people greedy or do we already have greedy people who use the economic freedom of the capitalistic system to achieve their ends? In light of the biblical description of human nature, the latter seems more likely.

Because people are sinful and selfish, some are going to use the capitalist system to feed their greed. But that is not so much a criticism of capitalism as it is a realization of the human condition. The goal of capitalism is not to change people but to protect us from human sinfulness.

Capitalism is a system in which bad people can do the least harm, and good people have the freedom to do good works. Capitalism works well if you have completely moral individuals. But it also functions adequately when you have selfish and greedy people.

Important to this discussion is the realization that there is a difference between self-interest and selfishness. All people have self-interest, and that can operate in ways that are not selfish. For example, it is in my self-interest to get a job and earn an income so that I can support my family. I can do that in ways that are not selfish.

Adam Smith recognized that every one of us has self-interest and rather than trying to change that, he made self-interest the motor of the capitalist system.

By contrast, other economic systems like socialism ignore the biblical definitions of human nature. Thus, they allow economic power to be centralized and concentrate power in the hands of a few greedy people. Those who complain of the influence major corporations have on our lives should consider the socialist alternative of how a few governmental bureaucrats control every aspect of their lives.

Greed certainly occurs in the capitalist system. But it does not surface just in this economic system. It is part of our sinfulness. Capitalism may have its flaws as an economic system, but it can be controlled to give us a great deal of economic prosperity and economic freedom.

CHAPTER 2 Ethics and Economics

What does the Bible have to say about economics? As we will see, the Bible does provide a firm moral foundation for economics. Previously we have talked about what the Bible has to say about economics. In this article we will discuss the ethical implications of economics, drawing many principles from the book *Bulls, Bears & Golden Calves* by John E. Stapleford.[2]

We should begin by establishing that there is a moral aspect to economics. This question was an important one a few centuries ago, but today economics is usually taught without any real consideration of an ethical component.

Paul says, "All Scripture is inspired by God and profitable for teaching, for reproof, for correction, for training in righteousness" (2 Tim. 3:16). He adds that this will enable the people of God to be equipped for every good work (2 Tim. 3:17). Certainly, that would include economic works.

James calls on believers to be "doers of the word, and not merely hearers" of the word (James 1:22). This command applies to more than just our church life and family life. This would apply to doing good works in the economic realm.

There are obvious moral implications to issues often discussed in relation to economic issues. Drugs, gambling, pornography are just a few examples. Christians should also learn to be good stewards of the environment. Each of these topics has an economic component to it, and thus implies that we should

---

[2] John Stapleford, *Bulls, Bears & Golden Calves* (Downers Grove, IL: 2002).

apply ethics to economics. Legalizing drugs has economic consequences, but it also has moral consequences as well.

Biblical View of Private Property

What does the Bible say about property, and especially about private property? First, the Bible clearly teaches that everything in the world belongs to the Lord. Psalm 24:1 says, "The earth is the Lord's, and all it contains, the world, and those who dwell in it."

At the same time, the Bible also teaches that we are given dominion over the creation (Gen. 1:28). We are accountable to God for our stewardship of the resources.

Because God owns it all (Ps. 24:1), no one owns property in perpetuity. But the Bible does grant private property rights to individuals. One of the Ten Commandments prohibits stealing, thus approving of private property rights. The book of Exodus establishes the rights of property owners and the liabilities of those who violate those rights.[3] Financial restitution (Ex. 22) must be made to property owners in cases of theft or neglect. Physical force is allowed to protect property (Ex. 22:2). Lost animals are to be returned, even when they belong to an enemy (Ex. 23:4). Removing landmarks that protect property is clearly forbidden (Deut. 19:14; 27:17; Job 24:2; Prov. 22:28; Hos 5:10).

Some Christians have suggested that the New Testament rejects the idea of private property because the book of Acts teaches that the early Christians held property in common. But this communal sharing in the New Testament was voluntary. Acts 2:44-47 says, "And all those who had believed were together and had all things in common; and they began selling their property

---

[3] Ibid., 63.

and possessions and were sharing them with all, as anyone might have need. Day by day continuing with one mind in the temple, and breaking bread from house to house; they were taking their meals together with gladness and sincerity of heart, praising God and having favor with all the people. And the Lord was adding to their number day by day those who were being saved."

The early Christians did not reject the idea of private property. Notice that they still retained private property rights until they voluntarily gave up those rights to help other believers in Jerusalem. This was a specific leading of the Holy Spirit to meet the increasing needs of the growing New Testament church.

We can see that they retained property rights in the actions of Ananias and Sapphira. Their sin was not that they retained control of some of their property but that they lied about it. Acts 5:4: "While it remained unsold, did it not remain your own? And after it was sold, was it not under your control? Why is it that you have conceived this deed in your heart? You have not lied to men but to God."

Also, notice that Paul called for voluntary charity toward believers in Jerusalem when he called New Testament believers to give to the needs of those within the church. 2 Corinthians 8:13-15 says, "For this is not for the ease of others and for your affliction, but by way of equality—at this present time your abundance being a supply for their need, so that their abundance also may become a supply for your need, that there may be equality; as it is written, 'He who gathered much did not have too much, and he who gathered little had no lack.'"

Biblical View of Work

What is the place of work in economic activity? First, we see that God put Adam and Eve in the Garden of Eden to work. God commanded them to work it and take care of it (Gen. 2:15-17). They were given an explicit command to exercise stewardship over the creation.

However, when sin entered the world, God's curse brought toil, sweat, and struggle to work (Gen. 3:17-19). But we still maintain the responsibility to work the land and cultivate it. We are also given the privilege by God of enjoying the earth and deriving profit and benefit from what it might produce (Gen. 9:1-3).

Second, we are created in God's image (Gen. 1:27), so we can find work rewarding and empowering. At the same time, we should also be held accountable for the work we do or fail to do. Paul says, "If a man will not work, he shall not eat" (2 Thess. 3:10, NIV).

Third, there is also a satisfaction in work. It not only satisfies a basic human need but it also is a privilege provided by the hand of God. Ecclesiastes 2:24 says, "There is nothing better for a man than to eat and drink and tell himself that his labor is good. This also I have seen that it is from the hand of God."

Fourth, we are to work unto the Lord. Paul admonishes believers to "work heartily as for the Lord rather than for men" (Col. 3:23). He also says, "For consider your calling, brethren, that there were not many wise according to the flesh, not many mighty, not many noble; but God has chosen the foolish things of the world to shame the wise, and God has chosen the weak things of the world to shame the things which are strong, and the base things of the world and the despised God has chosen, the things that are not, so that He may nullify the things that are, so that no man may boast before God. But by His doing you are in Christ Jesus, who became to us wisdom from God, and righteousness and sanctification, and redemption, so that, just as it is written, 'Let him who boasts, boast in the Lord'" (1 Cor. 1:26-31).

We also learn from Scripture that without God's involvement in our work, human labor is futile. Psalm 127:1 says, "Unless the Lord builds the house, they labor in vain who build it." God's blessings come to us through our labors.

Finally, with work there should also be rest. The law of the Sabbath (Ex. 20:8-11) and the other Old Testament provisions for feasts and rest demonstrate the importance of rest. In the New Testament also we see that Jesus set a pattern for rest (Mark 6:45-47; Luke 6:12) in His ministry. Believers are to work for the Lord and His Kingdom, but they must also avoid being workaholics and take time to rest.

Biblical View of Government

What is the role of government in the economic arena? First, Christians are commanded to obey government (Rom. 13:1) and submit to civil authority (1 Pet. 2:13–17). We are called to render service and obedience to the government (Matt. 22:21). However, we are not to render total submission. There may be a time in which Christians may be called to disobey government leaders who have set themselves in opposition to divine law (Rom. 13:1-5; John 19:11). We are to obey civil authorities (Rom.13:5) in order to avoid anarchy and chaos, but there may be times when we may be forced to obey God rather than men (Acts 5:29).

Second, we understand that because of the fall (Gen. 3), all have a sin nature (Rom. 3:23). Government must, therefore, administer justice in the political and economic realm. It must also protect us against aggression as well as provide for public works (1 Kings 10:9).

The reality of sin nature dictates that we not allow a political concentration of power. Governmental power should be limited to appropriate checks and balances.

Government also should not be used in a coercive way to attempt to change individuals. We should not accept the idea that the state can transform people from the outside. Only the gospel can change people from the inside and so that they become new creatures (2 Cor. 5:17).

In his book *Bulls, Bears & Golden Calves*, John E. Stapleford sets forth many functions of government in the economic realm. Government must ensure justice in the following ways:

- "Weights and scales are to be honest, a full measure (shaken down) is to be given (Lev. 19:35-36; Deut. 25:15; Prov. 20:23; Lk. 6:38), and currency is not be debased by inflationary monetary policy or other means (e.g., mixing lead with silver)."[4]

- Procedural justice requires that contracts and commitments be honored (Lev. 19:13).

- Government must also ensure justice when people are cheated or swindled. In these cases, the cost of restoration should be borne by the guilty or negligent party (Ex. 21:33-36; 22:5-8, 10-15). Government should also deal with those who give a false accusation (Deut. 19:16-19).

- Government should also prevent economic discrimination. This would apply to those of different economic class (James 2:1-4) as well as to those of different sex, race, and religious background (Gal. 3:26-29). Government can exert a great influence on the economy and therefore should use its regulatory power to protect against discrimination.

- That being said, the primary function of government is to set the rules and provide a means of redress. The free market should be allowed to function

---

[4] Ibid., 83.

with government providing the necessary economic boundaries and protections. Once this is done in the free enterprise system, individuals are free to use their economic choices in a free market.

Conclusion

What is the connection between economics and ethics? The fact that we even refer to these as separate issues is an indication of the times in which we live. In the past, ethics and economics were interconnected.

Thomas Aquinas, in his *Summa Theologica*, addressed economic issues in a moral and theological way. He wouldn't just ask about prices and markets, but also asked the fundamental question, What is a just price?

John Calvin's *Institutes of the Christian Religion* also devoted whole sections to government and economics. These were issues that he believed Christian theologians should address.

Today if moral questions about economics are discussed at all, they might be discussed in a class on economic theory. While we might hope that such discussions might surface in a seminary, usually those classes focus on theological questions rather than economic questions that deserve a moral reflection.

We have shown that economic issues often have a moral component. You can't just talk about the economic consequences of legalizing drugs, promoting pornography, or promoting gambling without dealing with the moral consequences.

We have also seen that the Bible has a great deal to say about work. Through the creation and the fall, human beings have a right and an obligation to work.

We find that the Bible also warns us of the consequences of idleness. Proverbs 24:30-34 says, "I passed by the field of the sluggard and by the vineyard of the man lacking sense, and behold, it was completely overgrown with thistles; Its surface was covered with nettles and its stone wall was broken down. When I saw, I reflected upon it; I looked, and received instruction. A little sleep, a little slumber, A little folding of the hands to rest, Then your poverty will come as a robber and your want like an armed man."

People are supposed to work and should be held accountable for the work they do or fail to do. Paul says, "If a man will not work, he shall not eat" (2 Thess. 3:10, NIV).

The Bible also teaches that God has endowed individuals with different gifts and talents (1 Cor. 12, Rom. 12). Even within the body of Christ, there are different members even though we are all one body in Christ.

When these differences in gifts and abilities are expressed within a free market, their respective value in terms of supply and demand means that they will receive different remuneration (1 Tim. 5:18). So it is not surprising that there are economic distinctions among individuals. Proverbs 22:2 says, "The rich and the poor have a common bond, The Lord is the maker of them all."

Ethics and economics are related, and Christians would be wise to begin exploring the moral implications of economic behavior and the impact it is having on them and society.

SECTION 2 Economic Systems

CHAPTER 3 Capitalism and Socialism

Americans traditionally have supported capitalism over socialism, but there is growing evidence that might be changing. A few polls show that just a mere majority of Americans say capitalism is better than socialism. America may not be ready to reject capitalism for socialism, but this poll does show less enthusiasm than in the past.

Age is a significant component. If you look at adults under the age of thirty in the poll, you find they are essentially evenly divided. More than a third of young people (thirty-seven percent) prefer capitalism, another third (thirty-three percent) embrace socialism, and the rest (thirty percent) are undecided.

What are we to make of this? First, the terms capitalism and socialism usually aren't defined in these polls. I suspect that if the pollsters explained the various tenets of socialism that the percentages would change. Defining capitalism would also be important since many would not necessary associate it with a free market but instead might have visions of an evil, greedy capitalist. After all, that is how many businessmen are portrayed in the media.

How should we define capitalism and socialism? Here are some brief definitions of these two economic systems. Capitalism is an economic system in which there is private property, and the means of production are privately owned. In capitalism, there is a limited role for government. Socialism is an economic system in which there is public or state ownership of the means of production, and the primary focus is on providing an equality of outcomes. In socialism, the state is all-important and involved in central planning.

Another question surfacing from these polls concerns those under the age of thirty. They are probably the least likely to associate socialism with Soviet-style repression. Instead, they may have in their minds the current government push toward European socialism and find that more attractive. Also, they are less likely to have "skin in the game." When you ask investors this same question about capitalism and socialism, they favored capitalism by a five-to-one margin.

Political affiliation is another determinant of support for capitalism. Republicans favor capitalism over socialism by an eleven-to-one margin. By contrast, Democrats are more closely divided. They barely favor capitalism (thirty-nine percent) over socialism (thirty percent).

The War Over Capitalism

As mentioned, many polls show that a slight majority of Americans say capitalism is better than socialism. This is hardly a strong endorsement of free market economics.

We might wonder if the percentages of support for these economic systems might change if different words were used. A survey taken in 2007 came to a different conclusion. The Pew Research Center asked people if they were better off "in a free market economy even though there may be severe ups and downs from time to time." In that case, seventy percent agreed, versus twenty percent who disagreed.[5] This might suggest that Americans like terms like "free market" more than "capitalism."

These polls illustrate that we are in the midst of a cultural conflict over capitalism. That is the conclusion of

---

[5] "World Publics Welcome Global Trade — But Not Immigration," Pew Research Center, 4 October 2007.

Arthur Brooks. His op-ed in *The Wall Street Journal* argues that "The Real Culture War is Over Capitalism."[6] He noted that President Obama's tax plan would increase the percentage of American adults who pay no federal income tax from forty percent to forty-nine percent (and another eleven percent will pay less than five percent of their income in tax). This has the potential to change attitudes about taxes since half of America won't be paying taxes.

Brookes says, "To put a modern twist on the old axiom, a man who is not a socialist at 20 has no heart; a man who is still a socialist at 40 either has no head or pays no taxes. Social Democrats are working to create a society where the majority are net recipients of the 'sharing economy.' They are fighting a culture war of attrition with economic tools."[7]

These various polls, as well as the current debate about the role of government in the economy, illustrate why we need to educate adults and young people about economics and the free market. How can we use biblical principles to evaluate economic systems like capitalism and socialism? The Bible does not endorse a particular system, but it does have key principles about human nature, private property rights, and the role of government. These can be used to evaluate economic systems.

The Bible warns us about the effects of sinful behavior in the world. Therefore, we should be concerned about any system that would concentrate economic power and thereby unleash the ravages of sinful behavior on the society. We should reject socialism

---

[6] Arthur Brooks, "The Real Culture War is Over Capitalism," The Wall Street Journal, 30 April 2009.
[7] Ibid.

and state-controlled economies that would concentrate power in the hands of a few sinful individuals.

Economic Criticisms

People often reject the idea of capitalism because they believe one of the *economic* criticisms of capitalism. Here are two of these criticisms.

The first economic criticism is that capitalism leads to monopolies. These develop for two reasons: too little government and too much government. Monopolies have occurred in the past because government has not been willing to exercise its God-given authority. Government finally stepped in and broke up the big trusts that were not allowing the free enterprise system to function correctly.

But in recent decades, the reason for monopolies has often been too *much* government. Many of the largest monopolies today are government-sanctioned or -sponsored monopolies that prevent true competition from taking place. The solution is for government to allow a freer market where competition can take place.

Let me add that many people often call markets with limited competition "monopolies" when the term is not appropriate. For example, the major car companies may seem like a monopolies or oligopolies until you realize that in the market of consumer durables the true market is the entire western world.

The second criticism of capitalism is that it leads to pollution. In a capitalistic system, pollutants are considered externalities. The producer will incur costs that are external to the firm so often there is no incentive to clean up the pollution. Instead, it is dumped into areas held in common such as the air or water.

The solution, in this case, is governmental regulation. However, this need not be a justification for building a massive bureaucracy. We need to find creative ways to direct self-interest so that people work towards the common good.

Sometimes when speaking on the topic of government and the environment, I use a thought experiment. Most communities use the water supply from a river and dump treated waste back into the water to flow downstream. Often there is a tendency to cut corners and leave the waste treatment problem for those downstream. But imagine if you required that the water intake pipe is downstream, and the waste pipe is upstream. If you did require this (and this is only a thought experiment), you would instantly guarantee that you would have less of a problem with water pollution. Why? It is now in the self-interest of the community to clean the wastewater being pumped back into the river.

We can acknowledge that although there are some valid economic criticisms of capitalism, these can be controlled by limited governmental control. And when capitalism is wisely controlled, it generates significant economic prosperity and economic freedom for its citizens.

Moral Criticism

Another reason people often reject the idea of capitalism is because they believe it is *immoral*. One of the moral arguments against capitalism involves the issue of greed. And this is why many Christians feel ambivalent towards the free enterprise system. After all, some critics of capitalism contend that this economic system makes people greedy.

To answer this question we need to resolve the following question: Does capitalism make people greedy

31

or do we already have greedy people who use the economic freedom of the capitalistic system to achieve their ends? In light of the biblical description of human nature, the latter seems more likely.

Because people are sinful and selfish, some are going to use the capitalist system to feed their greed. But that is not so much a criticism of capitalism as it is a realization of the human condition. The goal of capitalism is not to change people but to protect us from human sinfulness.

Capitalism is a system in which bad people can do the least harm, and good people have the freedom to do good works. Capitalism works well if you have completely moral individuals. But it also functions adequately when you have selfish and greedy people.

Important to this discussion is the realization that there is a difference between self-interest and selfishness. All people have self-interests that can operate in ways that are not selfish. For example, it is in my self-interest to get a job and earn an income so that I can support my family. I can do that in ways that are not selfish.

Capitalism was founded on the observation that all of us have self-interest. Rather than trying to change that, economists saw that self-interest could be the motor of the capitalist system.

By contrast, other economic systems like socialism ignore the biblical definitions of human nature. Thus, they allow economic power to be centralized and concentrate power in the hands of a few greedy people. Those who complain of the influence major corporations have on our lives should consider the socialist alternative of how a few governmental bureaucrats control every aspect of their lives.

Greed certainly occurs in the capitalist system. But it does not surface just in this economic system. It is part of our sinfulness. Capitalism may have its flaws as an economic system, but it can be controlled to give us a great deal of economic prosperity and economic freedom.

The Zero-Sum Myth

There is a myth that is often at the very foundation of many of the criticisms of capitalism. We can call it the zero-sum myth. By zero-sum, I mean that one person wins, and another person loses. Most competitive games are zero-sum games. One team or person wins; the other loses.

In most cases, the free market can be a win-win scenario rather than a win-lose scenario. In his book, *Money, Greed, and God*, Jay Richards uses a fun example from his childhood to illustrate this point.[8]

In the sixth grade, his teacher had them play the "trading game." She passed out little gifts to all of the students: a ten-pack of Doublemint gum, a paddleboard with a rubber ball, a Bugs Bunny picture frame, an egg of Silly Putty, a set of Barbie trading cards, etc.

She then asked the students to rate how much they liked their gift on a scale from one to ten. Then she compiled the score and put it on the board. Then she divided the class into five groups of five students and told them they could trade their gift with anyone in the group. Jay traded the Barbie trading cards he had with a girl in his group who had the paddleboard.

Then the teacher asked them to rate how much they liked their gifts. And she put that number on the board. The total score went up.

---

[8] Jay Richards, Money, Greed, and God (NY: Harper One, 2009), 60-61.

Then she told the students they could trade with anyone in the room. Now they had twenty-four possible trading partners rather than just the four in their group. The trading really began to take off. Once again, the teacher asked them to rate their gifts. When she put the number on the board, the total score went up again.

Almost everyone ended up with a toy he or she liked more than when the trading began. In fact, the only individual scores that did not go up were from students who really liked the gift they received initially from the teacher.

The students that day learned some valuable lessons about a free economy. When people are free to trade, they can add value to the traded item even though it remained physically unchanged. And they saw the value of having more trading partners (in this case twenty-four rather than four). Most of all, they learned that the free exchange could be a win-win proposition.

We can certainly admit that sometimes capitalism is not a win-win proposition. When there are limited resources and an individual or corporation is able to manipulate the political system in their favor, it is a win for the manipulator but a loss for Americans who did not have such political access. However, that is not a flaw in capitalism, but what results when government is corrupt or is corrupted by those who manipulate the system

CHAPTER 4 Hayek and the Road to Serfdom

A few years ago, if you said the name Friedrich Hayek to the average person in society, they wouldn't know his name. They might wrongly guess that he was the father of actress Selma Hayek. His name was unknown to non-economists.

Today he has much more visibility. People are reading his classic book, *The Road to Serfdom*, perhaps in order to make sense of our troubled economic climate and the current administration's policies. When TV host Glenn Beck talked about Hayek and *The Road to Serfdom*, the book went to number one on Amazon and stayed in the top ten for some time. A rap video featuring versions of Hayek and John Maynard Keynes have been viewed over a million times on YouTube.

Why all the interest in a Vienna-born, Nobel Prize-winning economist who passed off the scene some time ago? People are taking a second look at Hayek because of our current economic troubles. Russ Roberts, in his op-ed, "Why Friedrich Hayek is making a Comeback,"[9] says people are reconsidering four ideas Hayek championed.

First, Hayek and his fellow Austrian School economists such as Ludwig Von Mises argued that the economy is much more complicated than the simple economic principles set forth by Keynes. Boosting aggregate demand by funding certain sectors with a stimulus package of the economy won't necessarily help any other sector of the economy.

Second, Hayek highlighted the role of the Federal Reserve in the business cycle. The artificially low-interest

---

[9] Russ Roberts, "Why Friedrich Hayek is Making a Comeback," Wall Street Journal, 28 June 2010.

rates set by the Fed played a crucial role in inflating the housing bubble. Our current monetary policy seems to be merely postponing the economic adjustments that must take place to heal the housing market.

Third, Hayek argued in his book that political freedom and economic freedom are connected and intertwined. The government in a centrally controlled economy controls more than just wages and prices. It inevitably infringes on what we do and where we live.

Even when the government tries to steer the economy in the name of the "public good," the increased power of the state corrupts those who wield that power. "Hayek pointed out that powerful bureaucracies don't attract angels—they attract people who enjoy running the lives of others. They tend to take care of their friends before taking care of others."[10]

A final point by Hayek is that order can emerge not just from the top down but also from the bottom up. At the moment, citizens in many of the modern democracies are suffering from a top-down fatigue. A free market not only generates order but the freedom to work and trade with others. The opposite of top-down collectivism is not selfishness but cooperation.

Although *The Road to Serfdom* was written at the end of World War II to warn England that it could fall into the same fate as Germany, its warning to every generation is timeless.

---

[10] Ibid.

CHAPTER 5 Misconceptions About The Road to Serfdom

Hayek wrote his classic book *The Road to Serfdom*[11] more than sixty years ago, yet people are still reading it today. As they read it and apply its principles, many others misunderstand. Let's look at some of the prevalent misconceptions.

Because Hayek was a Nobel-winning economist, people wrongly believe that *The Road to Serfdom* is merely a book about economics. It is much more. It is about the impact a centrally planned socialist society can have on individuals. Hayek says one of the main points in his book is "that the most important change which extensive government control produces is a psychological change, an alteration in the character of the people. This is necessarily a slow affair, a process which extends not over a few years but perhaps over one or two generations."[12]

The character of citizens is changed because they have yielded their will and decision-making to a totalitarian government. They may have done so willingly in order to have a welfare state. Or they may have done so unwillingly because a dictator has taken control of the reins of power. Either way, Hayek argues, their character has been altered because the control over every detail of economic life is ultimately control of life itself.

In the forward to his book, Hayek makes his case about the insidious nature of a soft despotism. He quotes

---

[11] F.A. Hayek, The Road to Serfdom: Text and Documents, the Definitive Edition, ed. Bruce Caldwell (Chicago: University of Chicago Press, 2007).

[12] Ibid., 48.

from Alexis de Tocqueville's prediction in *Democracy in America* of the "new kind of servitude" when after having thus successively taken each member of the community in it powerful grasp, and fashioned him at will, the supreme power then extends its arm over the whole community. It covers the surface of society with a network of small, complicated rules, minute and uniform, through which the most original minds and the most energetic characters cannot penetrate to rise above the crowd. The will of man is not shattered but softened, bent and guided; men are seldom forced by it to act, but they are constantly restrained from acting. Such a power does not destroy, but it prevents existence, and stupefies a people, till each nation is reduced to be nothing more than a flock of timid and industrious animals, of which the government is the shepherd.[13]

Tocqueville warned that the search for greater equality typically is accompanied by greater centralization of government with a corresponding loss of liberty. The chapter was insightfully titled, "What Sort of Despotism Democratic Nations Have to Fear."

Tocqueville also described the contrast between democracy and socialism:

Democracy extends the sphere of individual freedom; socialism restricts it. Democracy attaches all possible value to each man; socialism makes each man a mere agent, a mere number. Democracy and socialism have nothing in common but one word: equality. But notice the difference: while democracy seeks equality in liberty, socialism seeks equality in restraint and servitude.[14]

Hayek believed that individual citizens should develop their own abilities and pursue their own dreams.

---

[13] Ibid., 49.

[14] Ibid., 77.

He argued that government should be a *means*, a mere *instrument*, "to help individuals in their fullest development of their individual personality."[15]

Some believe that Hayek was arguing that the road to socialism was inevitable. Actually, he was writing to predict a possible future for England based upon the past experience in Germany. He acknowledged that "although history never quite repeats itself, and just because no development is inevitable, we can in a measure learn from the past to avoid a repetition of the same process."[16] He did not argue that it was inevitable. In fact, he argued just the opposite. "Nor am I arguing that these developments are inevitable. If they were, there would be no point in writing this."[17]

Another misconception about Hayek is that he was making a case for radical libertarianism. Some of the previous quotes illustrate that he understood that the government could and should intervene in circumstances. He explains that his book was not about whether the government should or should not act in every circumstance.

What he was calling for was a government limited in scope and power. On the one hand, he rejected libertarian anarchy. On the other hand, he devoted the book to the reasons why we should reject a pervasive, centrally controlled society advocated by the socialists of his day. He recognized the place for government's role.

The government, however, should focus its attention on setting the ground rules for competition rather than devote time and energy to picking winners and losers in the marketplace. And Hayek reasoned that government cannot possibly know the individual and

---

[15] Ibid., 115.

[16] Ibid., 57.

[17] Ibid., 59.

collective needs of society. Therefore, Hayek argues that the "state should confine itself to establishing rules applying to general types of situations and should allow the individuals freedom in everything which depends on the circumstances of time and place because only the individuals concerned in each instance can fully know these circumstances and adapt their actions to them."[18]

Wise and prudent government must recognize that there are fundamental limitations in human knowledge. A government that recognizes its limitations is less likely to intervene at every level and implement a top-down control of the economy.

One last misconception has to do with helping those who suffer misfortune. It is true that he rejected the idea of a top-down, centrally controlled economy and socialist welfare state. But that did not exclude the concept of some sort of social safety net.

In his chapter on "Security and Freedom" he says, "there can be no doubt that some minimum of food, shelter, and clothing, sufficient to preserve health and the capacity to work can be assured to everybody."[19] He notes that this has been achieved in England (and we might add in most other modern democracies).

He went on to argue that the government should provide assistance to victims of such "acts of God" (such as earthquakes and floods). Although he might disagree with the extent governments today provide ongoing assistance for years; Hayek certainly did believe there was a place for providing aid to those struck by misfortune.

Paved With Good Intentions

---

[18] Ibid., 59.
[19] Ibid., 148.

Friedrich Hayek wrote *The Road to Serfdom* to warn us that sometimes the road can be paved with good intentions. Most government officials and bureaucrats write laws, rules, and regulations with every good intention. They desire to make the world a better place by preventing catastrophe and by encouraging positive actions from their citizens. But in their desire to control and direct every aspect of life, they take us down the road to serfdom.

Hayek says the problem comes from a "passion for conscious control of everything."[20] People who enter into government and run powerful bureaucracies are often people who enjoy running not only the bureaucracy but also the lives of its citizens. In making uniform rules from a distance, they deprive the local communities of the freedom to apply their own knowledge and wisdom to their unique situations.

Socialist government seeks to be a benevolent god but usually, morphs into a malevolent tyrant. Micromanaging the details of life leads to what Hayek calls "imprudence." Most of us would call such rules intrusive, inefficient, and often downright idiotic. But the governmental bureaucrat may believe he is right in making such rules, believing that the local people are too stupid to know what is best for them. Hayek argues that citizens are best served when they are given the freedom to make choices that are best for them and their communities.

Hayek actually makes his case for economic freedom using a moral argument. If government assumes our moral responsibility, then we are no longer free moral agents. The intrusion of the state limits my ability to make moral choices. "What our generation is in danger of forgetting is not only that morals are of necessity a

---

[20] Ibid.

phenomenon of individual conduct but also that they can exist only in the sphere in which the individual is free to decide for himself and is called upon voluntarily to sacrifice personal advantage to the observance of a moral rule."[21]

This is true whether it is an individual or a government that takes responsibility. In either case, we are no longer making free moral decisions. Someone or something else is making moral decisions for us. "Responsibility, not to a superior, but to one's conscience, the awareness of duty is not exacted by compulsion, the necessity to decide which of the things one values are to be sacrificed to others, and to bear the consequences of one's own decision, are the very essence of any morals which deserve the name."[22]

A socialist government may promise freedom to its citizens, but it adversely affects them when it frees them from making moral choices. "A movement whose main promise is the relief from responsibility cannot but be antimoral in its effect, however, lofty the ideals to which it owes its birth."[23]

Hayek also warned about the danger of centralizing power in the hands of a few bureaucrats. He argued that "by uniting in the hands of a single body power formerly exercised independently by many, an amount of power is created infinitely greater than any that existed before, so much more far-reaching as almost to be different in kind."[24]

He even argues that once we centralize power in a bureaucracy, we are headed down the road to serfdom.

---

[21] Ibid., 216.
[22] Ibid., 217.
[23] Ibid.
[24] Ibid., 165.

"What is called economic power, while it can be an instrument of coercion, is, in the hands of private individuals, never exclusive or complete power, never power over the whole of life of a person. But centralized as an instrument of political power it creates a degree of dependence scarcely distinguishable from slavery."[25]

Biblical Perspective

How does *The Road to Serfdom* compare to biblical principles? We must begin by stating that Friedrich Hayek was not a Christian. He did not confess Christian faith nor did he attend religious services. Hayek could best be described as an agnostic.

He was born in 1899 into an affluent, aristocratic family in Austria. He grew up in a nominally Roman Catholic home. Apparently, there was a time when he seriously considered Christianity. Shortly before Hayek became a teenager, he began to ask some of the big questions of life. In his teen years, he was influenced by a godly teacher and even came under the conviction of sin. However, his quest ended when he felt that no one could satisfactorily answer his questions. From that point on he seems to have set aside any interest in Christianity and even expressed hostility toward religion.

Perhaps the most significant connection between Hayek and Christianity can be found in their common understanding of human nature. Hayek started with a simple premise: human beings are limited in their understanding. The Bible would say that we are fallen creatures living in a fallen world.

Starting with this assumption that human beings are not God, he constructed a case for liberty and limited government. This was in contrast to the prevailing

---

[25] Ibid., 166.

socialist view that human beings possessed superior knowledge and could wisely order the affairs of its citizens through central planning. Hayek rejected the idea that central planners would have enough knowledge to organize the economy and instead showed that the spontaneous ordering of economic systems would be the mechanism that would push forward progress in society.

Hayek essentially held to a high view and a low view of human nature. Or we could call it a balanced view of human nature. He recognized that human beings did have a noble side influenced by rationality, compassion, and even altruism. But he also understood that human beings also are limited in their perception of the world and subject to character flaws.

Such a view comports with a biblical perspective of human nature. First, there is a noble aspect to human beings. We are created in the image of God (Gen. 1:27-28) and are made a little lower than the angels (Psalm 8:5). Second, there is a flaw in human beings. The Bible teaches that all are sinful (Rom. 3:23) and that the heart of man is deceitful above all things (Jer. 17:9).

Hayek believed that "man learns by the disappointment of expectations." In other words, we learn that we are limited in our capacities. We do not have God's understanding of the world and thus cannot effectively control the world like socialists confidently believe that we can. We are not the center of the universe. We are not gods. As Christians, we can agree with the concept of the "disappointment of expectations" because we are fallen and live in a world that groans in travail (Romans 8:22).

Although Hayek was not a Christian, many of the ideas in *The Road to Serfdom* connect with biblical principles. Christians would be wise to read it and learn from him the lessons of history.

CHAPTER 6 Wealth and Poverty

How should Christians think about wealth and poverty? Perhaps you have heard people say that money is evil, and that is why Christians must be poor. Actually, 1 Timothy 6:10 say that it is the "the love of money is a root of all sorts of evil."

Money can provide for your family, feed the poor, and promote the gospel. Of course, it can also be used to buy drugs, engage in prostitution, and ruin your life and the lives of others. So how should Christians think about wealth?

A Biblical View of Wealth

Our materialistic culture is seducing Christians into an economic lifestyle that does not glorify God. The popularity of television programs such as "Lifestyles of the Rich and Famous" and the veneration of social groups such as the glamorous "yuppies" testify to our society's materialistic values, values that many Christians have adopted.

Even within the Christian community, believers are bombarded with unbiblical views of wealth. At one extreme are those who preach a prosperity gospel of "health and wealth" for all believers. At the other extreme are radical Christians who condemn all wealth and imply that *rich Christian* is a contradiction in terms.

What, then, is the truly biblical view of wealth? At first glance, the Bible seems to teach that wealth is wrong for Christians. It appears even to condemn the wealthy. After all, both Jesus and the Old Testament prophets preached against materialism and seemed to say at times that true believers cannot possess wealth. If this is so,

45

then all of us in Western society are in trouble, because we are all wealthy by New Testament standards.

However, a comprehensive look at the relevant biblical passages quickly reveals that a biblical view of wealth is more complex. In fact, Scripture teaches three basic principles about wealth.

First, wealth itself is not condemned. For example, we read in Genesis 13:2 that Abraham had great wealth. In Job 42:10, we see that God once again blessed Job with material possessions. In Deuteronomy, Proverbs, and Ecclesiastes, wealth is seen as evidence of God's blessing (Deut. 8; 28; Prov. 22:2; Eccles. 5:19).

However, even though wealth might be an evidence of God's blessing, believers are not to trust in it. Proverbs, Jeremiah, 1 Timothy, and James all teach that the believer should not trust in wealth but in God (Prov. 11:4; 11:28; Jer. 9:23; 1 Tim. 6:17; James 1:11; 5:2).

Second, when wealthy people in the Bible were condemned, they were condemned for the means by which their riches were obtained, not for the riches themselves. The Old Testament prophet Amos railed against the injustice of obtaining wealth through oppression or fraud (4:11; 5:11). Micah spoke out against the unjust scales and light weights with which Israel defrauded the poor (6:1). Neither Amos nor Micah condemned wealth *per se*; they only denounced the unjust means by which it is sometimes achieved.

Third, Christians should be concerned about the effect wealth can have on our lives. We read in Proverbs 30:8-9 and Hosea 13:6 that wealth often tempts us to forget about God. Wealthy believers may no longer look to God for their provision because they can meet their basic needs. We read in Ecclesiastes 2 and 5 that people who are wealthy cannot really enjoy their wealth. Even billionaires often reflect on the fact that they cannot really enjoy the wealth that they have. Moreover, Proverbs 28:11 and Jeremiah 9:23 warn that wealth often leads to pride and arrogance.

Therefore, the Bible does not condemn those who are wealthy. However, it does warn us that if God blesses us with wealth, we must keep our priorities straight and guard against the seductive effects of wealth.

A Biblical View of Poverty

The Bible classifies the causes of poverty into four different categories. The first cause of poverty is oppression and fraud. In the Old Testament (e.g., Prov. 14:31; 22:7; 28:15) we find that many people were poor because they were oppressed by individuals or governments. Many times, governments established unjust laws or debased the currency, measures that resulted in the exploitation of individuals.

The second cause of poverty is misfortune, persecution, or judgment. In the book of Job, we learn that God allowed Satan to test Job by bringing misfortune upon him (1:12-19). Elsewhere in the Old Testament (e.g., Ps. 109:16; Isa. 47:9; Lam. 5:3), we read of misfortune or of God's judgment on a disobedient people. When Israel turned from God's laws, God allowed foreign nations to take them into captivity as a judgment for their disobedience.

The third cause of poverty is laziness, neglect, or gluttony. Proverbs teaches that some people are poor because of improper habits and apathy (10:4; 13:4; 19:15; 20:13; 23:21).

The final cause of poverty is the culture of poverty. Proverbs 10:15 says, "The ruin of the poor is their poverty." Poverty breeds poverty, and the cycle is not easily broken. People who grow up in an impoverished culture usually lack the nutrition and the education that would enable them to be successful in the future.

Poverty and Government

While government should not have to shoulder the entire responsibility for caring for the poor, it must take the statements seriously in Leviticus and Proverbs about defending the poor and fighting oppression. Government must not shirk its God-given responsibility to defend the poor from injustice. If government will not do this, or if the oppression is coming from the government itself, then Christians must exercise their prophetic voice and speak out against governmental abuse and misuse of power.

Government must first establish laws and statutes that prohibit and punish injustice. These laws should have significant penalties and be rigorously enforced so that the poor are not exploited and defrauded. Second, government must provide a legal system that allows for the redress of grievances where plaintiffs can bring their case to court for settlement.

A second sphere for governmental action is in the area of misfortune. Many people slip into poverty through no fault of their own. In these cases, government must help to distribute funds. Unfortunately, the track record of government programs is not very impressive. Before the implementation of many of the Great Society programs, the percentage of people living below the poverty level was 13.6 percent. Twenty years later, the percentage was still 13.6 percent.

We need a welfare system that emphasizes work and initiative and does not foster dependency and laziness. One of the things integral to the Old Testament system and missing in our modern system of welfare is a means test. If people have true needs, we should help them. But when they are lazy and have poor work habits, we should admonish them to improve. Our current welfare system perpetuates poverty by failing to distinguish between those who have legitimate needs and those who need to be admonished in their sin.

Poverty and the Church

The church has the potential to offer some unique solutions to poverty. Yet ever since the depression of the 1930s and the rise of the Great Society programs in the 1960s, the church has tended to abdicate its responsibility toward the poor to the government.

In the Old Testament, there were two means to help the poor. The first was through the gleaning laws listed in Leviticus 19:9-10 and Deuteronomy 24:19-22. As farmers reaped their crops, they would leave the corners of their fields unharvested, and anything that fell to the ground was left for the poor.

The second method used to help the poor was the tithe. In Leviticus 27:30 we find that the tithe provided funds both for the church and for the poor. The funds were distributed by the priests to those who were truly needy.

In the New Testament, the church also had a role in helping to meet the needs of the poor. In 1 Corinthians 16, Paul talks about a collection that was sent from the churches to the Jerusalem believers. We also find many scriptural admonitions calling for Christians to distribute their resources to others compassionately (2 Cor. 9:7; 1 Tim. 5:9-10; 6:18; James 1:27).

These verses concerning the gleaning laws and the tithe seem to indicate that both the government and the church should be involved in helping the poor. Ideally, the church should be in the vanguard of this endeavor.

Unfortunately, the church has neglected its responsibility, and government is now heavily involved in poverty relief.

I believe poverty relief should be a cooperative effort between the government and the church. As I noted above, government can provide solutions to exploitation and oppression by passing and enforcing just laws. It can also provide solutions to economic misfortune through various spending programs. But it cannot solve the problems of poverty by addressing injustice and misfortune alone. Poverty is as much a psychological and spiritual problem as it is an economic problem, and it is in this realm that the church can be most effective. Although salvation is not the sole answer, the church is better equipped than the government to meet the psychological and spiritual needs of poverty-stricken people. Most secular social programs do not place much emphasis on these needs and thus miss an important element in the solution to poverty.

Breaking the Cycle of Poverty

As I stated earlier, one of the causes of poverty is the culture of poverty. People are poor because they are poor. An individual who grows up in a culture of poverty is destined for a life of poverty unless something rather dramatic takes place. Poor nutrition, poor education, poor work habits, and poor family relationships can easily condemn an individual to perpetual poverty.

Here is where the church can provide some answers. First, in the area of capital investment, churches should develop a mercies fund to help those in need. Christians should reach out to those in poverty by distributing their own financial resources and by supporting ministries working in this area. Such an outreach provides churches with a mechanism to meet the physical needs of the poor as well as a context to meet their spiritual needs.

A second solution is for Christians to use their gifts and abilities to help those caught in the web of poverty. Doctors can provide health care. Educators can provide literacy and remedial reading programs. Businesspeople can impart job skills.

This kind of social involvement can also provide opportunities for evangelism. Social action and evangelism often work hand in hand. When we meet people's needs, we often open up opportunities to reach them for Jesus Christ.

This leads to a third solution. Christian involvement can lead to spiritual conversion. By bringing these people into a relationship with Jesus Christ, we can break the culture of poverty. Second Corinthians 5:17 says that we become new creatures in Jesus Christ. Being born again can improve attitudes and family relationships. It can give new direction and the ability to overcome handicaps and hardships.

The fourth area of Christian involvement is to call people to their biblical task. Proverbs 6:6 says, "Go to the ant, you sluggard, observe her ways and be wise"; we see here that we are to admonish laziness and poor habits that lead to poverty. In the New Testament, Paul reminds the Thessalonians of their church rule: "If a man will not work, he shall not eat" (2 Thess. 3.10). Christians should gently but firmly admonish those whose poverty is the result of poor work habits to begin taking responsibility for their own lives.

The church can help those addicted to alcohol or other drugs to overcome their dependencies. Christians can work to heal broken families. Dealing with these root causes will help solve the poverty problem.

The Christian Lifestyle

What, then, does this biblical view of wealth and poverty have to say about the way Christians should live? A brief survey of Scripture shows godly people living in a variety of different economic situations. For example, Daniel served as secretary of state in pagan administrations, and no doubt lived an upper-middle-class lifestyle. Ezekiel lived outside the city in what might have been considered a middle-class lifestyle. And Jeremiah certainly lived a lower-class lifestyle.

Which prophet best honored God with his lifestyle? The question is, of course, ridiculous. Each man honored God and followed God's leading in his life. Yet each lived a very different lifestyle.

Christians must reject the tacit assumption implicit in many discussions about economic lifestyle. There is no ideal lifestyle for Christians. One size does not fit all. Instead, we must seek the Lord to discern His will and calling in our lives.

As we do this, there are some biblical principles that will guide us. First, we should acknowledge that God is the Creator of all that we own and use. Whether we are rich or poor, we must acknowledge God's provision in our lives. We are stewards of the creation; the earth is ultimately the Lord's (Ps. 24:1).

Second, we should "seek first His kingdom and His righteousness" (Matt. 6:33). We must recognize and avoid the dangers of wealth. Greed is not an exclusive attribute of the rich, nor is covetousness an exclusive attribute of the poor. Christians must guard against the effect of wealth on their spiritual lives. There is nothing wrong with owning possessions. The problem comes when the possessions own us.

Third, Christians must recognize the freedom that comes with simplicity. A simple lifestyle can free us from the dangers of being owned by material possessions. It can also free us for a deeper spiritual life. While simplicity is not an end in itself, it can be a means to a spiritual life of service.

Here are a few suggestions on how to begin living a simple lifestyle. First, eat sensibly and eat less. This includes not only good nutrition but occasional times for prayer and fasting. Use the time saved for prayer and meditation on God's word. Use the money saved for world hunger relief.

Second, dress modestly. This not only obeys the biblical injunction of dressing modestly but avoids the Madison Avenue temptation of having to purchase new wardrobes as styles change. A moderate and modest wardrobe can endure the drastic swings in fashion.

Third, give all the resources you can. This includes both finances and abilities.

The famous Methodist preacher John Wesley had a simple recipe for a proper biblical perspective on money: earn all you can, save all you can, and give all you can.

- Concerning earning, Wesley said: "Gain all you can by honest industry. Use all possible diligence in your calling. Lose no time. If you understand yourself and your relation to God and man, you know you have none to spare."

- On saving money, he said: "Do not waste any part of so precious a talent merely in gratifying the desire of the eye by superfluous or expensive apparel, or by needless ornaments."

- He also admonished us to be generous in our giving. If we merely hoarded our money, he said: "You may as well throw your money into the sea, as bury it in the earth. And you may as well bury it in the earth, as in your chest, or in the Bank of England."[26]

Look for opportunities to give the resources God has blessed you with. If God has blessed you with wealth, look for opportunities to give it away prudently. If God has blessed you with great abilities, use them for His glory.

---

[26] John Wesley, "The Use of Money," The Sermons of John Wesley Thomas Jackson, ed., 1872 edition, http://wesley.nnu.edu/john_wesley/sermons/050.htm.

CHAPTER 7 Debt and Credit

We have been looking at biblical principles concerning economics and finances, but we also need to put the problem of debt in perspective. You cannot overemphasize the impact of debt on our society. It is the leading cause of divorce and also the reason for many more troubled marriages. It is also one of the causes of depression as well as suicide. People in debt didn't start out to ruin their lives and the lives of their families, but the consequences are often devastating.

The Bible has quite a bit to say about money and a significant part of these financial warnings concern debt. Proverbs 22:7 says, "The rich rule over the poor, and the borrower is a servant to the lender." When you borrow money and put yourself in debt, you put yourself in a situation where the lender has significant influence over you.

Many other verses in Proverbs also warn about the potential danger of debt (Proverbs 1:13-15; 17:18; 22:26-27; 27:13). While this does not mean that we can never be in debt, it does warn us about its dangers.

Romans 13:8 is an often misunderstood verse because it says, "Owe nothing to anyone." Although some theologians have argued that this verse prohibits debt, the passage needs to be seen in context. This passage is not a specific teaching about debt, but rather a summary of our duty as Christians to governmental authority. We should not owe anything to anyone (honor, taxes, etc.).

The Bible is filled with passages that provide guidelines to lending and borrowing. If debt was always wrong, then these passages would not exist, and there would be a clear prohibition against debt. But the implication of Romans 13:8 seems to be that we should pay our debts off a quickly as possible.

At this point, it would be good to make a distinction between debt and credit. Often in our society, the two words are used interchangeably. To put it simply, debt is something that is owed. The Bible does not prohibit borrowing, but it certainly does not recommend it. Credit is the establishment of mutual trust between a lender and borrower.

At the outset, let me acknowledge that some people end up in debt due to no fault of their own. They may have been swindled in a business. They may have made a good faith attempt to start a business but were unsuccessful because their competitions or suppliers cheated them. They may have been unfairly sued in court. The reasons are many.

The Consequences of Debt

What are the consequences of debt? The Bible describes debt as a form of slavery. Proverbs 22:7 says: "The rich rule over the poor, and the borrower is a servant to the lender." The borrower becomes a servant (or slave) to the person who is the lender.

If you look in the Old Testament, you will notice that debt was often connected to slavery. For example, both debts and slavery were canceled in the years of Jubilee. Sometimes people even put themselves in slavery because of debt (Deut. 15:2, 12).

Today we may not be in actual slavery from debt, but it may feel like it sometimes. We have all heard the phrase, "I owe, I owe, so it's off to work I go." If you are deep in debt, you know that there may be very few days off and perhaps no vacation. Someone in debt can begin to feel like a slave.

How can you know if you are too far in debt? Here are a few questions to ask yourself. Do you have an increasing collection of past-due bills on your desk? Do you drive down the road hoping you will win the lottery? Do you feel stress every time you think about your finances? Do you avoid answering the phone because you think it might be a collection agency? Do you make only minimum payments on credit cards?

One of the consequences of debt is we often deny reality. In order to realistically deal with the debt in our lives we need to get rid of some of the silly ideas running around in our heads.

For example, you are *not* going to win the lottery. Your debt problem is *not* going to go away if you just ignore it. And a computer glitch in your lender's computer is *not* going to wipe out your financial records accidentally so that you don't have to repay your debt.

Another consequence of debt is a loss of integrity. When we cannot pay, we start saying "the check's in the mail" when it isn't. We not only kid ourselves but we try to mislead others about the extent of our problem with debt.

Sometimes debt even leads to dishonesty. Psalm 37:21 says, "The wicked borrows and does not pay back." We should repay our debts.

A third consequence of debt is addiction. Debt is addictive. Once in debt, we begin to get comfortable with cars, consumer goods, furniture, etc., all funded through debt. Once we reach that comfort level, we go into further debt.

A final consequence of debt is stress. Stress experts have calculated the impact of various stress factors in our lives. Some of the greatest sources of stress are death of a spouse and divorce. But it is amazing how many other stress factors are financially related (change in financial

57

state, mortgage over $100,000). When we owe more than we can pay, we worry and feel a heavy load of stress that wouldn't exist if we lived debt free.

Credit Card Debt

To listen to the news reports, you would think that Americans are drowning in debt, but the story is not that simple. The latest economic statistics say that the average U.S. household has more than $9,000 in credit card debt. The average household also spends more than $1,300 a year in interest payments.

While these numbers are true, they are also misleading. The average debt per American household with at least one credit card is $9,000. But nearly one-fourth of Americans don't even own credit cards.

An even more telling fact is that more than thirty percent of American households paid off their most recent credit cards bills in full. So actually a majority of Americans owe nothing to credit card companies. Of the households that do owe money on credit cards, the median balance was $2,200. Only about 1 in 12 American households owe more than $9,000 on credit cards.

The $9,000 figure comes from CardWeb. It takes the outstanding credit card debt in America and divides it by the number of households that have at least one credit card. While the average is accurate, it is misleading.

Liz Pulliam Weston, writing for MSN Money, explains: "The example I usually give to illustrate the fallacy of averages is to imagine that you and 17 of your friends were having dinner with Bill Gates and Warren Buffett. The average net worth of a person at that table would be about $5 billion. The fact that everybody else's personal net worth was a lot less wouldn't affect the average that much because Bill and Warren are so much wealthier than the rest of us."[27]

Yes, Americans are in debt. And some Americans are really in debt. If you are one of those individuals, you should apply the biblical principles we are discussing to your situation. If you are not in debt, learn a vicarious lesson about what can happen if you don't pay attention to debt.

Here are some principles for dealing with credit card debt. First, realize that the problem is not the credit card in your hand. The problem may be with the person holding the credit card. Proverbs 22:3 says, "The prudent sees the evil and hides himself, but the naïve go on, and are punished for it."

Second, never use credit cards except for budgeted purchases. Impulse shopping with credit cards is one of the major reasons people find themselves in debt.

Third, pay off your credit cards every month. If you cannot pay off your credit card bill, don't use your credit card again until you can pay your bill.

Home Mortgage

Most Christian financial counselors put a home mortgage in a different category than other debt. There are a number of reasons for this.

First, a home loan is secured by the equity in the home. After an initial down payment, a loan schedule (of principle and interest) is applied to the balance of the home expense. If a homeowner faces a financial crisis, he or she can sell the house and use that amount to retire the loan.

---

[27] Liz Pulliam Weston, "The big lie about credit card debt," MSN Money, 30 July 2007, tinyurl.com/33zrut.

Second, a home is often an appreciating asset. In many housing markets, the price of a home increases every year. This makes it an even less risky financial investment. But of course, what goes up can also go down. Some homeowners have seen the value of their home decrease significantly. That affects their ability to repay their home loan if they need to sell their house.

Third, a home mortgage is a tax deduction and thus provides a small financial benefit to homeowners that they would not have if they were renting. At the same time, eager homebuyers shouldn't over-estimate the value of this and justify buying a home that is beyond their means.

Fourth, the interest in a home loan is usually within a few percentage points of the prime rate. This means that the interest rate on a typical home loan is about one-third the interest rate of a typical credit card.

While a home mortgage may be different from other forms of debt, that doesn't mean there aren't dangers and pitfalls. As we have already mentioned, people buy homes assuming that they will appreciate in value. But many find that the house prices stagnate or even decline. After paying closing costs, they may owe more on their home loan than they received from the sale of their house.

Another concern about a home mortgage is that many homeowners end up buying more house than they can really afford. Just because they qualify for a particular house doesn't mean they should buy a house that will stretch them financially.

Changing financial circumstances may surprise a couple that qualifies for a house mortgage. For example, the wife may get pregnant and no longer be able to work and provide the income necessary to make the monthly mortgage payment. Either partner might get laid

60

off from work and not provide the necessary income. And there are always unexpected expenses for homeowners (new furnace, hot water heater, etc.) that couples may not have budgeted for when they purchased a home.

One formula that is often used in considering a home mortgage is to buy a home that is less than two and a half times a family's annual gross income. Another is to consider what you can currently pay in rent and compare that amount to the home mortgage (plus the additional expenses such as insurance, taxes, etc.). The two amounts should be similar.

Getting Out of Debt

Let us conclude by talking about how to get out of debt. If you are already in debt, you need to break the debt cycle with discipline applied over time.

First, establish the right priorities. God owns it all. Unfortunately, we often believe that we own it all. We need to transfer ownership of all our possessions mentally to God (Psalm 8). This would also include giving the Lord His part and honoring Him with your giving (even if it is a small amount).

Second, stop borrowing. If a pipe broke in your house, the first thing to you would do is shut off the water before you started to mop up the water. Before you do anything else, "shut off" the borrowing. Don't use your credit card. Don't take out a bank loan.

Third, develop a budget. This is something you might do by yourself or with the help of many online ministries and financial services, that provides guidelines. On the other hand, you may consult with a financial expert who can give you guidelines.

You would begin by making a list of all of your monthly expenses (mortgage or rent, utilities, groceries, car payments, credit card bills, etc.). Then you need to establish a priority for the loans that you have that are outstanding. This should include information about the amount owed and the interest rates. Then you need to set aside a realistic budget that allows you to have enough money to pay off the loans in a systematic way.

Write to each creditor with a repayment plan based upon this realistic budget. It might be good even to include a financial statement and a copy of your budget so they can see that you are serious about getting out of debt.

Fourth, begin to retire your debt. If you can, pay extra on the debts with the highest interest rates. If all of them have comparable interest rates, you might instead pay extra on the smallest balance. By paying that off first, you will have a feeling of accomplishment and then free up some of your income to tackle your next debt.

Fifth, develop new spending habits. For example, if you generate extra income from working overtime or at an extra job, use that to retire your debt faster. Don't assume that because you have some extra discretionary income you can use that to spend it on yourself.

Before you buy anything, question yourself. If an item is not in your budget, ask yourself if you really need it and how much use you will get out of it. We often spend because we are used to spending. Change your spending habits.

Debt is like a form of slavery. Do what you can to be debt free. If you follow these steps faithfully, that can take place in a few years. Debt freedom will reduce your stress and free you up to accomplish what God intends for you to do.

SECTION 3 Challenges in the 21st Century

CHAPTER 8 Is the World Flat?

Is the world flat? The question is not as crazy as it might sound in light of the book by Thomas Friedman entitled *The World is Flat: A Brief History of the Twenty-First Century*. His contention is that the global playing field has been leveled or flattened by new technologies.

In fourteen hundred and ninety-two when Columbus sailed the ocean blue, he used rudimentary navigational equipment to prove that the earth was *round*. More than 500 years later, Friedman discovered in a conversation with one of the smartest engineers in India that essentially the world was *flat*. Friedman argues that we have entered into a third era of globalization, which he calls Globalization 3.0 that has flattened the world.

The first era of globalization (he calls Globalization 1.0) lasted from when Columbus set sail until around 1800. "It shrank the world from a size large to a size medium. Globalization 1.0 was about countries and muscles."[28] The key change agent in this era was how much muscle your country had (horsepower, wind power, etc.). Driven by such factors as imperialism and even religion, countries broke down walls and began the process of global integration.

The second era (he calls Globalization 2.0) lasted from 1800 to 2000 with interruptions during the Great Depression and World Wars I and II. "This era shrank the world from size medium to a size small. In Globalization 2.0, the key agent of change, the dynamic force driving global integration, was multinational companies."[29] At first these were Dutch and English joint-stock companies,

---
[28] Thomas Friedman, The World is Flat: A Brief History of the Twentieth Century (New York: Farrar, Straus and Giroux, 2005), 9.
[29] Ibid.

64

and later was the growth of a global economy due to computers, satellites, and even the Internet.

The dynamic force in Globalization 1.0 was *countries* globalizing, while the dynamic force in Globalization 2.0 was *companies* globalizing. Friedman contends that Globalization 3.0 will be different because it provides "the newfound power for *individuals* to collaborate and compete globally."[30]

The players in this new world of commerce will also be different. "Globalization 1.0 and 2.0 were driven primarily by European and American individuals and businesses. . . . Because it is flattening and shrinking the world, Globalization 3.0 is going to be more and more driven not only by individuals but also by a much more diverse—non-Western, non-white—group of individuals. Individuals from every corner of the flat world are being empowered."[31]

The Flatteners

Friedman argues in his book that the global playing field has been flattened by new technologies.

The first flattener occurred on November 9, 1989. "The fall of the Berlin Wall on 11/9/89 unleashed forces that ultimately liberated all the captive peoples of the Soviet Empire. But it actually did so much more. It tipped the balance of power across the world toward those advocating democratic, consensual, free-market-oriented governance, and away from those advocating authoritarian rule with centrally planned economies."[32]

The economic change was even more important. The fall of the Berlin Wall encouraged the free movement of ideas, goods, and services. "When an

---
[30] Ibid., 10.
[31] Ibid., 11.
[32] Ibid., 49.

economic or technological standard emerged and proved itself on the world stage, it was much more quickly adopted after the wall was out of the way."[33]

Thomas Friedman also makes a connection between the two dates 11/9 and 9/11. He noted that in "a world away, in Muslim lands, many thought [Osama] bin Laden and his comrades brought down the Soviet Empire and the wall with religious zeal, and millions of them were inspired to upload the past. In short, while we were celebrating 11/9, the seeds of another memorable date—9/11—were being sown."[34]

A second flattener was Netscape. This new software played a huge role in flattening the world by making the Internet truly interoperable. Until then, there were disconnected islands of information.

We used to go to the post office to send mail; now most of us send digitized mail over the Internet known as *e-mail*. We used to go to bookstores to browse and buy books; now we browse digitally. We used to buy a CD to listen to music, now many of us obtain our digitized music off the Internet and download it to an MP3 player.

A third flattener was workflow software. As the Internet developed, people wanted to do more than browse books and send e-mail. "They wanted to shape things, design things, create things, sell things, buy things, keep track of inventories, do somebody else's taxes, and read somebody else's X-rays from half a world away. And they wanted to be able to do any of these things from anywhere to anywhere and from any computer to any computer—seamlessly."[35]

---

[33] Ibid., 52.

[34] Ibid., 55.

[35] Ibid., 73.

All the computers needed to be interoperable not only between departments within a company but between the systems of any other company. Workflow software made this possible.

Where will this lead? Consider this likely scenario. When you want to make a dentist appointment, your computer translates your voice into a digital instruction.

Then it will check your calendar against the available dates on the dentist's calendar. It will offer you three choices, and you will click on the preferred date and hour. Then a week before your appointment, the dentist's calendar will send you an e-mail reminding you of the appointment. The night before your appointment, a computer-generated voice message will remind you.

The fourth flattener is open-sourcing. Open-source comes from the idea that groups would make available online the source code for software and then let anyone who has something to contribute improve it and let millions of others download it for free.

One example of open-source software is Apache, which currently powers about two-thirds of the websites in the world. Another example of open-sourcing is blogging. Bloggers are often one person online commentators linked to others by their common commitments. They have created an open-source newsroom essentially.

News bloggers were responsible for exposing the bogus documents use by CBS and Dan Rather in a report about President Bush's Air National Guard service. Howard Kurtz of *The Washington Post* wrote (Sept 20, 2004): "It was like throwing a match on kerosene-soaked wood. The ensuing blaze ripped through the media establishment as previously obscure bloggers managed to put the network of Murrow and Cronkite on the defensive."

Another example of open-sourcing is the Wikipedia project which has become perhaps the most popular online encyclopedia in the world. Linux is another example. It offers a family of operating systems that can be adapted to small desktop computers or laptops all the way up to large supercomputers.

A fifth flattener is outsourcing. In many ways, this was made possible when American companies laid fiber-optic cable to India. Ultimately, India became the beneficiary.

India has become very good at producing brain power, especially in the sciences, engineering, and medicine. There are a limited number of Indian Institutes within a population of one billion people. The resulting competition produces a phenomenal knowledge meritocracy. Until India was connected, many of the graduates would come to America. "It was as if someone installed a brain drain that filled up in New Delhi and emptied in Palo Alto."[36]

Fiber-optic cable became the ocean crosser. You no longer need to leave India to be a professional because you can plug into the world from India.

A sixth flattener was offshoring. Offshoring is when a company takes one of its factories that is operating in Canton, Ohio and moves the whole factory to Canton, China.

When China joined the World Trade Organization, it took Beijing and the rest of the world to a new level of offshoring. Companies began to shift production offshore and integrate their products and services into their global supply chains.

The more attractive China makes itself offshoring, the more attractive other developed and developing

---

[36] Ibid., 105.

countries have to make themselves. This created a process of competitive flattening and a scramble to give companies the best tax breaks and subsidies.

How does this affect the United States? "According to the U.S. Department of Commerce, nearly 90 percent of the output from U.S.-owned offshore factories is sold to foreign consumers. But this actually stimulates American exports. There is a variety of studies indicating that every dollar a company invests overseas in an offshore factory yields additional exports for its home country, because roughly one-third of global trade today is within multi-national companies."[37]

The seventh flattener is supply chaining. "No company has been more efficient at improving its supply chain (and thereby flattening the world) than Wal-Mart, and no company epitomizes the tension the supply chains evoke between the consumer in us and the worker in us than Wal-Mart."[38]

Thomas Friedman calls Wal-Mart "the China of companies" because it can use its leverage to grind down any supplier to the last halfpenny. And speaking of China, if Wal-Mart were an individual economy, it would rank as China's eighth-biggest trading partner, ahead of Russia, Australia, and Canada.

An eighth flattener is what Friedman calls *insourcing*. A good example of this is UPS. UPS is not just delivering packages; the company is doing logistics. Their slogan is "Your World Synchronized." The company is synchronizing global supply chains.

For example, if you own a Toshiba laptop computer under warranty that you need fixed, you call Toshiba. What you probably don't know is that UPS will pick up

---

[37] Ibid., 123.
[38] Ibid., 129.

your laptop and repair it at their own UPS-run workshop dedicated to computer and printer repair. They fix it and return it in much less time than it would take to send it all the way to Toshiba.

A ninth flattener is in-forming. A good example of that is Google. Google has been the ultimate equalizer. Whether you are a university professor with a high-speed Internet connection or a poor kid in Asia with access to an Internet café, you have the same basic access to research information.

Google puts an enormous amount of information at our fingertips. Essentially, all of the information on the Internet is available to anyone, anywhere, at any time.

Friedman says that "In-forming is the ability to build and deploy your own personal supply chain—a supply chain of information, knowledge, and entertainment. In-forming is about self-collaboration—becoming your own self-directed and self-empowered researcher, editor, and selector of entertainment, without having to go to the library or movie theater or through network television."[39]

A tenth flattener is what he calls "the steroids." These are all the things that speed the process (computer speed, wireless). For example, the increased speed of computers is dazzling. The Intel 4004 microprocessor (in 1971) produced 60,000 instructions per second. The Intel Pentium 4 Extreme has a maximum of 10.8 billion instructions per second.

The wireless revolution allows anyone portable access to everything that has been digitized anywhere in the world. When I was in graduate school at Yale University, all of us were tied to a single mainframe computer. In order to use the computer, I had to hand computer cards to someone in the computer lab in order to input data or extract information. Now thanks to

---

[39] Ibid., 153.

digitization, miniaturization, and wireless I can do all of that and much more from my home, office, coffee shop, or airport.

Biblical Perspective

Although futurists have long talked about globalization and a global village, many of these forces have made that a reality. At this point, it might be valuable to distinguish between *globalization* and *globalism*. Although these terms are sometimes used interchangeably, I want to draw some important distinctions. Globalization is used to describe the changes taking place in society and the world due to economic and technological forces. Essentially, we have a global economy and live in the global village.

Globalism is the attempt to draw us together into a new world order with a one world government and one world economy. Sometimes this even involves a desire to develop a one-world religion. There certainly are legitimate concerns about this push towards global government. We should be concerned about political attempts to form a new world order.

On the other hand, we should also recognize that globalization is already taking place. *The World is Flat* focuses on many of the positive aspects of this phenomenon, even though there are many critics would believe it might be harmful.

Some believe that it will benefit the rich at the expense of the poor. Some believe it will diminish the role of nations in deference to world government. These are important issues that we will attempt to address in future articles.

For now, let us look at some important implications of a flat world. First, we should prepare our children and grandchild for global competition. Thomas Friedman says that when he was growing up his parents would tell him "Finish your dinner. People in China and India are starving." Today he tells his daughters, "Girls, finish your homework—people in China and India are starving for your jobs."[40]

Another implication is the growing influence of the two countries with the largest populations: China and India. Major companies are looking to these countries for research and development. The twentieth century was called "the American Century." It is likely that the twenty-first century will be "the Asian Century."

These two countries represent one-third of the world's population. They will no doubt transform the entire global economy and political landscape. Students of biblical prophecy wonder if these two countries represent the "Kings of the East" (Rev. 16:12). In the past, most of the focus was only on China. Perhaps the Kings (plural) represent both China and India.

A final implication is that this flattened world has opened up ministry through the Internet and subsequent travel to these countries. Probe Ministries, for example, now has a global ministry. In the past, it was the occasional letter we received from a foreign country. We now interact daily with people from countries around the world.

The flattening of the world may have its downsides, but it has also opened up a ministry in ways that were unimaginable just a few years ago. Welcome to the flat world.

---

[40] Ibid., 237.

CHAPTER 9 Globalization and the Wal-Mart Effect

In the previous chapter, we talked about global trade and the process of globalization as it related to the flat world. In this chapter, we will continue to look at that process by using Wal-Mart as an example of what is happening in our world. Thomas Friedman, in his book *The World is Flat*, says that if Wal-Mart were an individual economy, it would rank as China's eighth-biggest trading partner, ahead of Russia, Australia, and Canada.[41]

Throughout this chapter, we will be referring to many of the facts and figures from Charles Fishman's book *The Wal-Mart Effect*.[42] For example, he points out that more than half of all Americans live within five miles of a Wal-Mart store. For most people, that is about a ten- to fifteen-minute drive. Ninety percent of Americans live within fifteen miles of a Wal-Mart. In fact, when you drive down the interstate, it is rare for you to go more than a few minutes without seeing a Wal-Mart truck.

Wal-Mart has over 3800 stores in the United States. That is more than one Wal-Mart store for every single county in the country.[43] And they don't exactly fade into the landscape. They sit on vast aprons of asphalt parking and stand out because of their sheer size.

Wal-Mart has also become the national commons. Every seven days more than one hundred million Americans shop at Wal-Mart (that's one-third of the

---

[41] Thomas Friedman, The World is Flat: A Brief History of the Twentieth Century (New York: Farrar, Straus and Giroux, 2005), 137-138.

[42] Charles Fishman, The Wal-Mart Effect (New York: Penguin, 2006).

[43] Ibid., 6.

country). Each year, ninety-three percent of American households shop at least once at Wal-Mart. Their sales in the United States are more than $2000 per household. Wal-Mart's profit on that amount was just $75.00.[44]

The size of this company is hard to grasp. Wal-Mart is not just the largest retailer in the United States but rather in the world. For most of this decade, it has been both the largest company in the world as well as the largest company in the history of the world.

In 2006, Wal-Mart was to be bumped from the number-one spot on the Fortune 500 list of the largest companies by ExxonMobil, whose sales surged past Wal-Mart's because the world price of oil rose so much in the prior year. However, with the fall in oil prices over the past two years, well below $50.00 per barrel, Wal-Mart remains the number one largest company in the world.

However, if you consider payrolls, there is no comparison. ExxonMobil employs about 90,000 people worldwide. Wal-Mart employs 1.6 million.[45] And there's another difference. ExxonMobil is growing by raising prices. Wal-Mart is growing despite lowering prices.

Put another way; Wal-Mart is as big as Home Depot, Kroger, Target, Costco, Sears, and Kmart combined. Target might be considered Wal-Mart's biggest rival and closest competitor, but it is small in comparison. Wal-Mart sells more by St. Patrick's Day (March 17) than Target sells all year.[46]

The Wal-Mart Effect

Ask people to give you their opinion about Wal-Mart and you are likely to get lots of different responses.

---

[44] Ibid.
[45] Ibid., 7.
[46] Ibid.

They may talk with enthusiasm about the "always low prices." Or they might talk about the impact Wal-Mart had on small businesses in their community when the first store arrived. They may even talk about the loss of American jobs overseas. Believe me; most will have an opinion about Wal-Mart.

Wal-Mart had its creation in the mind of Sam Walton who promoted a single idea: sell merchandise at the lowest price possible. It began with Wal-Mart working hard to keep the costs of their company as low as possible. This idea moved from their company to their suppliers as they asked them to be as frugal as possible. As the company grew in size, they began looking for every way to wring out the last penny of savings from materials, packaging, labor, transportation, and display. The result was "the Wal-Mart effect."

Consumers have embraced "the Wal-Mart effect." As a store moves into a community bringing lower prices, it drives down prices in other stores. Either they compete or close their doors. It also reshapes the shopping habits of those in the community.

However, with "the Wal-Mart effect" comes fears of "the Wal-Mart economy." This is the nagging feeling that there are social and economic costs to be paid for "always low prices." Critics talk about low wages, minimal benefits, and little chance for career advancement.

The company has found itself under attack from many quarters. There is a lawsuit on behalf of 1.6 million women who have worked at Wal-Mart that alleges systematic sex discrimination. Add to this the allegations that managers have required employees to work off the clock and even have locked employees in stores overnight.

There is also the constant complaint that Wal-Mart does not provide adequate health care benefits. Last year, for example, the Maryland legislature passed a bill that forces companies with more than 10,000 employees to spend at least eight percent of their payroll on health care or pay the state the difference. Since Wal-Mart is the only employer with over 10,000 employees in the state, it is easy to see that the legislation was only targeting Wal-Mart.

Wal-Mart recently settled a federal investigation of its use of illegal aliens to clean its stores. The company made a record-setting payment to the federal government.

Sam Walton's goal from the beginning was an unrelenting focus on controlling costs in order to provide "always low prices." He instilled in his employees core values like hard work, frugality, discipline, and loyalty.[47]

In his book *The Wal-Mart Effect*, Charles Fishman says these values have become inverted. He points out how the company has changed. When Sam Walton died in 1992, Wal-Mart was a $44 billion-a-year company with 370,000 employees. The number of employees has now grown by 1.2 million, and sales have grown by $240 billion. "Wal-Mart is not only not the company Sam Walton founded; it is no longer the company he left behind."[48]

Out of the Box

You probably never thought about the packaging around deodorant, but Wal-Mart did. Until the early 1990s, nearly every brand of deodorant came in a paperboard box. Most consumers opened the box, pulled out the deodorant container, and tossed the box

---

[47] Ibid., 27.
[48] Ibid., 48.

into the garbage. Some of us recycled them, but we were a very small minority.

In the early 1990s, Wal-Mart (along with a few other retailers) decided the paperboard box was a waste. The product came in a can or plastic container. These were at least as tough as the box. The box took up wasted space, and it wasted cardboard. Shipping the weight of the cardboard added weight to trucks and wasted fuel. And the box itself cost money to design and produce. It even cost money to put the deodorant into the box.

Wal-Mart began to apply pressure on the suppliers to eliminate the box. Deodorant manufacturers calculated that the box cost about a nickel for every consumer. Wal-Mart split the savings. Deodorant makers keep a few pennies, and Wal-Mart passed a couple of pennies savings on to the consumers.

Walk into Wal-Mart today and look at the deodorant aisle. You will probably find eight shelves of deodorant, sixty containers across. In this sea of nearly five hundred containers of deodorant, not one box.

Consider the impact of this one decision. First, there is the environmental impact. Whole forests were not cut down to provide a box that consumers did not use. A few recycled them, but the vast majority threw them away seconds after they removed their deodorant. Was Wal-Mart's pressure to unbox deodorant a good thing? It certainly was, if you are concerned about environmental issues.

The economic impact was also considerable. A savings of one nickel might seem trivial until you multiply it by the two hundred million adults in the United States. If you just account for the container of deodorant in every American bathroom, you have a savings of $10 million, of which consumers got to keep half. But don't forget that the savings is recurrent. Americans are saving $5 million in nickels about five to six times a year.

But there is also a third impact. The impact this decision had on jobs. So far, the decision looks like a win-win. However, you might not feel so excited about the decision if you work in the forestry industry or are in the paperboard box business.

This story illustrates only so well the problem with providing a clear, unambiguous analysis of consumer behavior in American markets, even more so, the ethics of corporations in a global market. And this story is probably easier to analyze if your first priority is the environment. But the ethics of other situations that arise from globalization aren't quite so easy to evaluate.

Wal-Mart illustrates the world in which corporate entities significantly influence our decisions and even transform an economy. While we might like the outcome of saving paperboard boxes, we certainly don't like other aspects of "the Wal-Mart effect." The company has grown so large and evolved in unexpected ways that it is difficult to predict what the future holds. When we begin to ask moral questions, it isn't so easy to always determine whether the outcomes are good for the country and us.

Salmon

Americans love to eat salmon. In fact, we eat more than 1.75 million pounds of salmon a day.[49] We eat it at home and when we go out to a restaurant. Americans buy lots of cheap salmon from Wal-Mart. But they are probably unaware of the impact their purchase has on the environment. Most of the salmon served in the United States is Atlantic salmon (which is a species that is

---

[49] Ibid., 169.

not only found wild but is also the species of choice for salmon farmers).

The salmon that you buy in Wal-Mart is "a factory product." In other words, they are hatched from eggs, raised in freshwater hatcheries, and then grown to maturity in open-topped ocean cages in cold coastal waters.[50]

Wal-Mart sells more salmon than any other store in the country. Wal-Mart also buys all its salmon from Chile. In fact, they purchase about one-third of the annual harvest of salmon that Chile sells. Wal-Mart sells the salmon for $4.84 a pound. It seems incredible that they can sell it for so little, but there are hidden costs.

Atlantic salmon is not native to Chile (its coastline runs along the Pacific). It's an exotic species that is literally farmed and processed by thousands of Chileans. The labor conditions are certainly a concern (long hours, low pay, processing of salmon with razor-sharp filleting instruments).

Another concern is the environment. Salmon farming is already transforming the ecology of southern Chile "with tens of millions of salmon living in vast ocean corrals, their excess food and feces settling to the ocean floor beneath the pens, and dozens of salmon processing plants dumping untreated salmon entrails directly into the ocean."[51]

When we buy salmon from Chile, are we contributing to this environmental damage? Charles Fishman asks, "Does it matter that salmon for $4.84 a pound leaves a layer of toxic sludge on the ocean bottoms of the Pacific fjords of southern Chile?"[52] After

---

[50] Ibid., 170.
[51] Ibid., 171.
[52] Ibid., 172.

all, these salmon are raised in pens (with as many as one million per farm). They are fed antibiotics to prevent disease. As a result, you have quite a mess. One million salmon produce about the same amount of waste as 65,000 people. Add to that additional waste from unconsumed food and antibiotic residue. In essence, the current method of salmon farming creates a toxic seabed.

So how do we change this? The answer is simple: by changing consumer behavior. If shoppers won't buy salmon until Wal-Mart insists on higher standards, Wal-Mart will insist on them. The same company that created this huge market for salmon can also change it. But this will only happen if consumers voice their concerns and back it up with their behavior.

Consumer Behavior

As I said earlier, mention the name Wal-Mart and you are likely to get lots of varied reactions. While shoppers love the "always low prices," critics point to the impact that the company has had on the economy and the environment.

In fact, it is a bit misleading to think of Wal-Mart as merely a company. In reality, it is a global market force. Without a doubt, it is one of the most efficient entities at improving its supply chain not only in this country but also around the world. Most of us just shop at the store and do not think of the implications of what we buy and where we buy it.

The size of Wal-Mart gives it the power to do many positive things. It recently announced fuel-savings plans for its stores and trucks. This could provide a model for the nation.

Wal-Mart also provided a model of how to deal with a disaster like Hurricane Katrina. Even though they had 171 facilities in the path of the storm, they were able to recover and reopen eighty-three percent of their facilities in the Gulf area within six days.

One key to Wal-Mart's success is associates who are dedicated to their communities. The local connection helped it deliver goods when the government failed. Wal-Mart sprang into action even before the hurricane hit. Whenever there is a possibility of a hurricane, its supply chain automatically adjusts and sends in plenty of non-perishable food and generators.

What is Wal-Mart's effect on the local economy? One famous study found that the arrival of a Wal-Mart store had a dramatic impact. "Grocery stores lost 5 percent of their business, specialty stores lost 14 percent of their business, and clothing stores lost 18 percent of their business—all while total sales were rising 6 percent, mostly due to Wal-Mart."[53]

Critics of Wal-Mart say that it forces small businesses into bankruptcy. But if you think about it, it is the consumers who put people out of business. We vote with our wallets. Shoppers are the ones who have made it possible for Wal-Mart's phenomenal growth. And we are the ones who need to pay attention to what we buy and where we buy it.

Our consumer behavior can have a positive impact on our world. As individuals, we have a minimal impact, but collectively we have an impact on our lives and our economy every day when we spend money. For too long, Christians have been willing to separate ethics from economics. In earlier centuries, theologians asked important questions about the relationship of morality to money.

It is time to return to that moral reflection, especially in this age of globalization. Christians should be alert consumers in this global economy.

---

[53] Ibid., 156.

CHAPTER 10 Is America Broke?

Let me begin with a provocative question: Is America going broke? It is a question that has been asked many times before. When an economist asks the question, it creates quite a stir.

Back in 2006, Laurence Kotlikoff asked: "Is the United States Bankrupt?"[54] He concluded that countries can go broke and that the United States is going broke due to future obligations to Social Security and Medicare. At the time, his commentary generated lots of discussion and controversy.

Two years later that same economist writing for *Forbes* magazine asked the question in a slightly different way: "Is the U.S. Going Broke?"[55] He pointed out that the federal government's takeover of Fannie Mae and Freddie Mac represented a major financial challenge. These two institutions issue about half of the mortgages in America, so that part of the bailout put the government on the hook for $5 trillion (if you consider the corporate debt that is owed and the mortgage debt that is guaranteed).

However, $5 trillion is effectively pocket change when you consider the real liabilities that are facing our government. He estimates that is on the order of $70 trillion. I have seen others estimate our unfunded liabilities at anywhere from $50 trillion to as high as more than $90 trillion. Let's (for the sake of discussion) use the $70 trillion figure.

---

[54] Laurence Kotlikoff, "Is the United States Bankrupt?" Federal Reserve Bank of St. Louis Review, July/August 2006, 88(4), pp. 235-49.

[55] Laurence Kotlikoff, "Is the U.S. Going Broke?" Forbes, September 29, 2008

The $70 trillion figure actually represents the fiscal difference between the government's projected spending obligations and all its projected tax receipts. He notes, "This fiscal gap takes into account Uncle Sam's need to service official debt-outstanding U.S. government bonds. But it also recognizes all our government's unofficial debts, including its obligation to the soon-to-be-retired baby boomers to pay their Social Security and Medicare benefits."[56]

When we are talking about such large dollar amounts, it is hard to put this in perspective. Let's focus on the challenge that the baby boom generation creates. There are approximately 78 million baby boomers that will be retiring over the next few decades. Each of them can expect to receive approximately $50,000 each year (in today's dollars) during their retirement. OK, so let's multiply 78 million by a $50,000 annual payment and you get an annual cost of $4 trillion per year.

Of course, these are just the obligations we know about. There are others potential costs and obligations that aren't even calculated into the national debt. Housing prices certainly fit into that category. We know some of the obligations that were written into law but cannot predict what might take place in the future. And we don't know how many banks in the future will fail and what that cost might be to the American taxpayer.

Fannie Mae and Freddie Mac

If you asked most people what they know about Fannie Mae and Freddie Mac they would probably respond that they know very little about these two corporations. However, after the bailout in 2008, most Americans know a lot more about these two institutions.

---
[56] Ibid.

Fannie Mae is the Federal National Mortgage Association, and Freddie Mac is the Federal Home Loan Mortgage Corporation. They are stockholder-owned corporations and referred to as government-sponsored enterprises, known as GSEs. The two of them are considered the largest financial companies in the world with liabilities of approximately $5 trillion.

The bailout of these institutions was controversial for a few reasons. First, these two GSEs are private companies that the government wanted to help with taxpayer money. Economist John Lott believes "this whole approach is pretty dubious. If you subsidize risk, you get more of it. If you don't have to bear the cost of the risk, why not shoot for the moon?"

Former House Majority Leader Dick Armey said we were "privatizing gains while socializing losses." Stockholders of Fannie Mae and Freddie Mac already receive higher interest rates than Treasury securities because of higher risk of repayment. He suggests that the government repay 90 cents on the dollar rather than 100 percent.

In the midst of the debates about bailouts, we learned some vital lessons about the economy. For example, some have talked about the proposal to suspend the accounting rules of the Sarbanes-Oxley Act known as "mark to market." Trying to understand this proposal forced us to get up-to-speed on economics and accounting.

We also learned that sometimes a regulatory agency might not have done a good job warning us of dangers. The Office of Federal Housing Enterprise Oversight employs 200 people to oversee Fannie Mae and Freddie Mac, which are the government-sponsored, entities that own or guarantee nearly half of the nation's residential mortgages. Just a few months before the collapse of

Fannie and Freddie, the OFHEO issued a report that saw clear sailing ahead.

We also learned that in trying to do some good, government can do harm. During the 1990s the Treasury Department changed the lending rules for the Community Reinvestment Act. This was an attempt to get middle-income and low-income families into homes. Unfortunately, these families lacked the resources to make their payments. It was only a matter of time before many of those families defaulted on their loans.

Medicare

Usually, when we talk about unfunded liabilities, the conversation usually turns to Social Security. It turns out that the Social Security shortfall is a problem, but it pales in comparison to the shortfall for Medicare.

Medicare is a pay-as-you-go program. Although some members of Congress warned about future problems with the system, most politicians simply ignored the potential for a massive shortfall. Medicare comes in three parts. Medicare Part A covers hospital stays; Medicare B covers doctor visits, and Medicare D was recently added as a drug benefit.

How big is the financial shortfall? Let me quote from a speech given Richard Fisher (President and Chief Executive Officer, Federal Reserve Bank of Dallas). He says:

> The infinite-horizon present discounted value of the unfunded liability for Medicare A is $34.4 trillion. The unfunded liability of Medicare B is an additional $34 trillion. The shortfall for Medicare D adds another $17.2 trillion. The total? If you wanted to cover the unfunded liability of all three programs today, you would be stuck with an $85.6 trillion bill. That is more than six times as

large as the bill for Social Security. It is more than six times the annual output of the entire U.S. economy.[57]

There are a number of factors that contribute to this enormous problem. First, there are the demographic realities that are also affecting Social Security. From 1946 to 1964 we had a baby boom followed by a baby bust. Never has such a large cohort been dependent on such a small cohort to fund their entitlement programs. Second, there is longevity. People are living longer lives than ever before. Third, the cost of medical treatment and technology is increasing. We have better drugs and more sophisticated machines, but these all cost money. Finally, we have a new entitlement (the prescription drug program) that is an unfunded liability that is one-third greater than all of Social Security.

Richard Fisher says that if you add the unfunded liabilities from Medicare and Social Security, you come up with a figure that is near $100 trillion. "Traditional Medicare composes about 69 percent, the new drug benefit roughly 17 percent and Social Security the remaining 14 percent."[58]

So what does this mean to each of us? We currently have a population over 300 million. If we divide the unfunded liability by the number of people in America, the per-person payment will come to $330,000. Put another way; this would be a bill to a family of four for $1.3 million. That is over 25 times the average household's income.

---

[57] Richard W. Fisher, "Storms on the Horizon," remarks before the Commonwealth Club of California (San Francisco, CA, May 28, 2008).

[58] Ibid.

Consumer Debt

We have been answering the question, Is America Going Broke? Now I would like to shift the focus and ask a related question. Are Americans going broke? While government debt has been exploding, so has consumer debt.

Let us look at just a few recent statistics. Nearly half of all American families spend more than they earn each year. Personal bankruptcies are at an all-time high and increasing. It is estimated that consumers owe more than $2 trillion.

It is important to remember that although many Americans are significantly in debt, many others are not. In an earlier chapter on debt and credit, we pointed out how some of the statistics about credit card debt are misleading.

The current statistics say that the average U.S. household has more than $9,000 in credit card debt. We also read that the average household also spends more than $1,300 a year in interest payments. While these numbers are true, they are also misleading. The average debt per American household with at least one credit card is $9,000. But nearly one-fourth of Americans don't even own credit cards.

We should also remember that more than thirty percent of American households pay off their most recent credit cards bills in full. So actually a majority of Americans owe nothing to credit card companies. Of the households that do owe money on credit cards, the median balance was $2,200. Only about 1 in 12 American households owe more than $9,000 on credit cards.

The statistic is true but very misleading. That is also true of many other consumer debt statistics. For example, nearly two-thirds of consumer borrowing involves what

87

is called "non-revolving" debt such as automobile loans. Anyone who has ever taken out a car loan realizes that he or she is borrowing money from the bank for a depreciating asset. But it is an asset that usually has some resale value (unlike a meal or a vacation purchased with a credit card).

However, even in this case, the reality is different from perception. Yes, many families have car payments. But many other families do not have a car payment and owe nothing to the bank. So we have to be careful in how we evaluate various statistics about consumer debt.

The bottom line, however, is that government, families, and individuals are spending more than they have. Government is going broke. Families and individuals are going broke. We need to apply biblical principles to the subject of debt.

Biblical Perspective

Proverbs 22:7 says, "The rich rule over the poor, and the borrower is a servant to the lender." When you borrow money and put yourself in debt, you put yourself in a situation where the lender has significant influence over the debtor. This is true whether the debtor is an individual or an entire nation.

Many of the Proverbs also warn about the potential danger of debt (Proverbs 1:13-15; 17:18; 22:26-27; 27:13). While this does not mean that we can never be in debt, it does warn us about its dangers. It is never wise to go into debt, and many are now wondering if America and individual Americans are going broke.

Romans 13:8 says, "Owe nothing to anyone." This passage seems to indicate that we should quickly pay off our debts. That would imply that Christians have a duty to pay their taxes and pay off their debts.

But what should we do if government continues to get further and further in debt? I believe that we should hold government officials responsible since it appears that they do not have any real desire to pay off its debt. Psalm 37:21 says, "The wicked borrows and does not pay back." We should repay our debts as individuals, and government should pay its debts as well.

In the Old Testament, debt was often connected to slavery. Isn't it interesting that both debts and slavery were canceled in the year of Jubilee? It is also worth noting that sometimes people even put themselves in slavery because of debt (Deuteronomy 15:2, 12).

Since we live in the New Testament age, we do not have a year of Jubilee, but we need to hold government and ourselves accountable for debt. If we see a problem, we should address it immediately. Proverbs 22:3 says, "The prudent sees the evil and hides himself, but the naïve go on, and are punished for it." It is time for prudent people to take an honest appraisal of our financial circumstances.

When government is in debt this much, it really has only three options. It can raise taxes. It can borrow the money. Or it can print the money. While it is likely that government will raise taxes in the future, there does seem to be an upper limit (at least politically) to raising taxes. Borrowing is an option, but it is also unlikely that the U.S. government can borrow too much more from investors and other countries. That would suggest that the Federal Reserve will print more money, and so our money will be worth less.

In this chapter, we have given you an honest appraisal of where we are as a country. The responsibility is now in our hands to hold government accountable and to take the necessary steps in our own financial circumstances.

CHAPTER 11 Do We Have Financial Security?

What kind of financial security can you expect in the future? The answer to that question may depend on when you were born. The leading edge baby boomers will do much better than the generations following them.

A major reason is demographics. The baby boom was preceded, and more importantly, succeeded by consecutive years of fewer births. Thirty-five percent more Americans were born during the baby boom than during the previous nineteen years. And 12 percent more were born than during the subsequent nineteen years. This nineteen-year blip in fertility has created more than just an oddity in social statistics. It has clouded the financial future of most Americans.

The elderly are supported, especially during the waning years of their old age, by members of the younger generation. The baby boom was immediately followed by a baby bust, or what many commentators have labeled a "birth dearth." This disproportionate ratio between baby boomers and baby busters raises questions about the boom generation's future and suggests it will face an impending crisis of financial security.

Concern arises from both economic and demographic realities. The harsh economic reality is the federal deficit has now reached $20 trillion. Aggravating this economic situation are also such issues as trade deficits, increased taxes, higher oil prices, and an inevitable downturn in the economy.

The biggest issue isn't so much economics as it is how demographics affect economics. The sheer size of the boom generation has had a negative impact on its members. Paul Hewitt of the Retirement Policy Institute put it this way:

> The baby boom as a generation has been its own worst enemy. Whenever we wanted anything the price went up, and when we sold the price went down. So we got less for our labor and paid more for our houses. When we want to sell those houses the price will go down, and when we want medical care in old age, prices will go up.[59]

Many Americans find themselves part of what has become called "the triple-squeeze generation." Americans with elderly parents are finding that providing long-term care for parents is affecting their ability to save for their children's education and also affecting their ability to save for their own retirement.

Commentators have also referred to these people as the "sandwich generation" because they are sandwiched between an older generation dependent upon them for elder care and a younger generation dependent upon them for housing and education. The economic and demographic realities may seem dismal, but they will be much worse if we fail to apply biblical principles to our finances. The key to financial security for most Americans has been the three-legged stool of savings, pensions, and Social Security. Unfortunately, economic termites threaten the strength of that stool.

Savings

The first leg on the retirement stool is savings. The boomers are justly concerned about the savings (or more to the point, the lack of savings) they have put away so

---

[59] David Kirkpatrick, "Will You Be Able to Retire?" Fortune, 31 July 1989, 57.

far for their retirement. A survey of leading-edge boomers found that six out of ten expressed great concern about being able to meet all of their financial responsibilities, and 62 percent fear that they will outlive their retirement savings.

But they aren't the only ones concerned. A survey by the American Academy of Actuaries echoed boomers' fears. Seventy-two percent of pension-fund actuaries polled predicted that half the baby boom won't have the wherewithal to retire at age 65.[60]

How much have Americans saved so far? Well, not very much if a recent survey is any indication. A report by the Federal Reserve found that: "Forty-seven percent of respondents say they either could not cover an emergency expense costing $400, or would cover it by selling something or borrowing money."[61]

The inability of nearly a majority of Americans to come up with the sum of four hundred dollars illustrates two things. First, it shows how little (if anything) they have in savings or investments. Second, it demonstrates how much many of them are in debt. The first leg of the three-legged stool is in awful shape because, for many in the boom generation, savings are decreasing while debt is increasing.

The reasons for American debt are fairly simple. First, the boomers and busters had great expectations for themselves and were often willing to go deeply in debt in order to finance the lifestyle they had chosen for themselves. Second, they had the misfortune of entering the consumer world at the time when wages were stagnant and when most of the goods and services they

---

[60] Susan Dentzer, "How We Will Live," U.S. News and World Report, 25 Dec. 1989, 62.

[61] Report on the Economic Well-Being of U.S. Households in 2014, Board of Governors of the Federal Reserve System, May 2015.

craved were hit by inflation. This further fueled consumer borrowing; this became both a cause and a consequence of their downward mobility.

Families in debt usually are not saving. If they had any financial resources to save and invest, they would be wise to first retire their high-interest consumer debt. In 1984, more than a third of all households headed by a person under thirty-five had no savings whatsoever on deposit with banks and other financial institutions, aside from non-interest-paying checking accounts.

The solution to this problem is simple: Get out of debt and put money into savings and retirement. Now while this may be easy to say, it is difficult for the current generation to do. Baby boomers' expectations frequently exceed their income, and the changing economic and demographic realities place them in a precarious position. But if this generation wants to have a more secure financial future, it must take appropriate financial measures now.

Corporate Pensions

In the past, there used to be an unwritten agreement between a company and an individual. If you faithfully worked for the company, the company would take care of you in your retirement. But this tacit agreement has broken down for two reasons.

First, many of these companies lack the financial resources to take care of their retirees. Consolidation of some companies and the bankruptcies of many others put pensions in jeopardy. Other companies heavily invested in speculative schemes by thrifts and junk bonds, and their portfolios rest on shaky ground. In other cases, the current financial resources seem adequate but have yet to be tested when the millions of baby boomers begin to retire.

Second, most Americans have not spent enough time with any one company to earn a significant pension. It was not uncommon for the parents of baby boomers to have worked for a single company for more than twenty years. Baby boomers and the following generations, on the other hand, change jobs if not career paths with unprecedented frequency.

This apparent restlessness is born from both choice and necessity. Boomers are much less likely to stay in a job that does not enhance personal development and self-expression. Unlike their fathers and grandfathers, who would often remain with a company "for the sake of the family," the following generations are much more likely to move on.

Americans also change jobs out of necessity. They find themselves competing with each other for fewer upper-management positions for a number of reasons. First, companies have thinned their management ranks. Most of this restructuring was done in the 1980s to make companies more efficient. The rest was a natural result of buyouts, takeovers, and consolidation leaving fewer structural layers in upper management and fewer jobs.

All of these factors have put this generation in a precarious position. By and large, they are not saving and have inadequate pensions to give them a secure financial future. So many are trusting that Social Security will be there for them when they retire. But will it?

Social Security

The impending Social Security debacle is complex and the subject of whole books. But the basic issue can be illustrated by once again looking at the demographic impact of the boom generation.

When Social Security began in the mid-1930s, the ratio of workers to recipients was ten to one and life expectancy was two years below retirement age. The pay-as-you-go system could work with those kinds of numbers.

But two fundamental demographic changes threaten to send Social Security off a cliff. First is the "senior boom." Advances in modern medicine have raised life expectancy by 28 years in just this century. Today the median age is over 36 and still climbing. One has to wonder about the stability of Social Security in a country where each year an increasing percentage of Americans qualify for membership in the American Association of Retired Persons.

The second demographic change is the ratio between the baby boom generation and the baby bust generation. The smaller generation following the boom generation will have to support Social Security as more baby boomers retire. The system will face incredible strains through the next few decades as the ratio of workers to Social Security beneficiaries continues to decline.

Both demographic changes are relevant. Americans are living longer, and ratios between generations are skewed. These two changes are certain to transform the current pay-as-you-go system into nothing more than an elaborate Ponzi scheme by the twenty-first century.

The solutions to the Social Security crisis are few and all politically difficult to achieve. Either you have to change the supply of contributions or the demand of the recipients. Increasing the supply of contributors could be achieved by increasing the birth rate (unlikely, and probably too little too late). You could also allow more immigration of workers who could contribute to Social Security (but that has its own political issues).

95

The only other way to increase the supply of contributions is to increase FICA payments. But there will have to be an upper limit on how much Americans can be taxed. If benefits stay at their current levels, workers in the year 2040 could find Social Security taking as much as 40 percent of their paychecks.

Decreasing demand would require trimming benefits. Current recipients benefit most from Social Security. A retiree on Social Security today recovers everything he paid into the system in about four years. On the other hand, few boomers will ever get the amount of money they paid into the system. Some politicians have suggested trimming benefits to current recipients. Others suggest, applying a means test to wealthy recipients or those who receive other pension income. Neither proposal has much likelihood of passage.

More likely, Congress will be forced to trim future benefits. Congress has already increased the age of retirement and may induce workers to stay on the job until age 70. Another solution would be to provide the biggest tax breaks for workers to fund their own retirement through IRAs or Keoghs.

Obviously, the solutions are not popular, but the alternative is a collapse of the Social Security system in the next decade. If something isn't done, the demographic realities will destroy the system.

Retirement

Although this generation grew up assuming retirement would be the norm, the changing social and economic conditions we have discussed may force a rethinking of that basic assumption. After all, the idea of retirement historically is of recent origin.

When Social Security was first adopted in 1935, life expectancy was below 63, a full two years under the retirement age.[62] Retirement was for the privileged few who lived long enough to enjoy the meager financial benefits from the system.

Even as late as the 1950s, the contemporary image we have today of retirement communities and the elderly sightseeing in recreational vehicles did not exist. Retirement still did not exist as an institution. Nearly half the men over age 65 were still in the workforce.

Polls taken during the 1950s and early 1960s showed that most Americans desired to work for as long as they could and saw retirement merely for the disabled. Today, however, most Americans look forward to their retirement as a time to travel, pursue personal interests, and generally indulge themselves. Yet the demographic landscape suggests we might have to revise our current images of retirement.

As baby boomers slowly jog towards Golden Pond, they will likely be the largest generation of senior citizens in history, both in absolute size and in relative proportion to the younger generation. These large numbers will precipitate a "retirement crisis" for two reasons. First, people are living longer. We have raised the life expectancy by 28 years. During most of human history, only one in ten lived to the age of 65. Today eight out of every ten Americans zoom past their 65th birthday.

Second, the burden of providing retirement benefits will fall upon the younger, (and more to the point) smaller generation born after the baby boom. Never will so few be required to fund the retirement of so many. When Social Security was adopted in 1935, there were

---

[62] Ken Dychtwald and Joe Flowers, Age Wave: The Challenge and Opportunities of An Aging America (New York: Bantam, 1990), 66.

ten workers for every person over age 65. That ratio shrank to six to one in the 1970s.

Today there are about three working Americans to support each retiree. But by the time the last boomer hits retirement age in 2029, the ratio of workers to retirees will drop to less than two to one. Obviously, baby boomers face much greater uncertainty than their parents did when they entered into the years now seen as the time of retirement.

This next generation may even decide to reject the idea of retirement, choosing instead to enrich themselves with meaningful work all of their lives. Yet such an idyllic vision could quickly be crushed by the harsh reality of failing health. Working until you are 70 or beyond may not be physiologically possible for all people.

No wonder a chorus of Cassandras is predicting financial disaster in the next century. But significant changes can be made now to avert or at least lessen a potential crisis in the future. Wise investment according to biblical principles now is absolutely necessary to prepare for this uncertain future.

CHAPTER 12 Economics: Past and Future

Anyone watching the news or looking at his or her checking account knows that we are in for some tough economic times. Let's look at how we arrived at this place and set forth some biblical principles that we collectively and individually need to follow.

The Bailout

Who would have imagined a few decades ago America would spend such enormous amounts of money on a bailout? The first bailout was for $700 billion. When these numbers are so big, we lose all proportion of their size and potential impact. So let me use a few comparisons from a recent *Time* magazine article to make my point.[63]

If we took $700 billion and gave it to every person in America, they would receive a check for $2,300. Or if we decided to give that money instead to every household in America, they would receive $6,200.

What if we were able to use $700 billion to fund the government for a year? If we did so, it would fully fund the Defense Department, the State Department, the Treasury, the Department of Education, Veterans Affairs, the Department of the Interior, and NASA. If instead we decided to pay off some of the national debt, it would retire seven percent of that debt.

Are you a sports fan? What if we used that money to buy sports teams? This is enough money to buy every NFL team, every NBA team, and every Major League

---

[63] "What Else You Could Spend $700 Billion On," *Time*, September 2008,www.eandppub.com/2008/09/what-else-you-c.html.

Baseball team. However, we would have so much left over that we could also buy every one of these teams a new stadium. In addition, we would still have so much money left over that we could pay each of these players $191 million for a year.

Of course, this is just the down payment. When we add up all the money for bailouts and the economic stimulus, the numbers are much larger (some estimate on the order of $4.6 trillion).

Jim Bianco (of Bianco Research) crunched the inflation-adjusted numbers.[64] The last government bailout actually costs more than all of the following big budget government expenditures: the Marshall Plan ($115.3 billion), the Louisiana Purchase ($217 billion), the New Deal ($500 billion [est.]), the Race to the Moon ($237 billion), the Savings and Loan bailout ($256 billion), the Korean War ($454 billion), the Iraq war ($597 billion), the Vietnam War ($698 billion), and NASA ($851.2 billion).

Even if you add, all of this up, it actually comes to $3.9 trillion and so it is still $700 billion short (which incidentally is the original cost of one of the bailout packages most people have been talking about).

Keep in mind that these are inflation-adjusted figures. Therefore, you can begin to see that what has happened a few years ago was absolutely unprecedented. Until you run the numbers, it seems like Monopoly money. But the reality is that it is real money that must either be borrowed or printed. There is no stash of this amount of money somewhere that Congress is putting into the economy.

---

[64] Barry Ritholtz, "Big Bailouts, Bigger Bucks," Bailouts, Markets, Taxes and Policy,www.ritholtz.com/blog/2008/11/big-bailouts-bigger-bucks/.

What Caused the Financial Crisis?

What caused the financial crisis? First, there was risky mortgage lending. Some of that was due to government influence through the Community Reinvestment Act that encouraged commercial banks and savings associations to loan money to people in low-income and moderate-income neighborhoods. And part of it was due to the fact that some mortgage lenders were aggressively pushing subprime loans. Some did this by fraudulently overestimating the value of the homes or by overstating the lender's income. When these people couldn't pay on their loan, they lost their homes (and we had a record number of foreclosures).

Next, the lenders who pushed those bad loans went bankrupt. Then a whole series of dominoes began to fall. Government-sponsored enterprises like Fannie Mae and Freddie Mac as well as financial institutions like Bear Stearns, Lehman Brothers, Merrill Lynch and AIG began to fail.

As this was happening, commentators began to blame government, the financial institutions, Wall Street, and even those who obtained mortgages. Throughout the 2008 presidential campaign and for years after, there was a cry that this was the result of shredded consumer protections and deregulation.

So is the current crisis a result of these policies? Is deregulation the culprit? Kevin Hassett has proposed a simple test of this view.[65] He points out that countries around the world have very different regulatory structures. Some have relatively light regulatory structures, while others have much more significant intrusion into markets.

---

[65] Kevin Hassett, "The Regulators' Rough Ride," National Review, 15 December 2008, 10.

If deregulation is the problem, then those countries that have looser regulations should have a greater economic crisis. But that is not what we find. If you plot the degree of economic freedom of a country on the x-axis and the percent of change in the local stock market on the y-axis, you find just the opposite of that prediction.

The correlation is striking. Draw a line from countries with low economic freedom (like China and Turkey) to countries with greater economic freedom (like the United States) and you will notice that most of the countries hug the line. Put another way; the regression line is statistically significant.

If the crisis were a result of deregulation, then the line should be downward sloping (meaning that countries that are freer economically had the biggest collapse in their stock markets). But the line slopes up. That seems to imply that countries that are economically free have suffered less than countries that are not. While it may be true that a single graph and a statistical correlation certainly do not tell the whole story, it does suggest that the crisis was not due to deregulation.

The End of Prosperity

As the 2008 financial crisis was unfolding, a significant economic book was coming on the market. The title of the book is *The End of Prosperity* by Arthur Laffer, Stephen Moore, and Peter Tanous.[66] The book provides excellent documentation to many of the economic issues we have already discussed but also looks ahead to the future.

---

[66] Arthur Laffer, Stephen Moore, and Peter Tanous, The End of Prosperity (New York: Simon and Schuster, 2008).

The authors show that contrary to conventional wisdom, the middle class has been doing better in America. They show how people in high tax states are moving to low-tax states. And they document the remarkable changes in Ireland due to lowering taxes. I have talked about some of these issues in previous articles and in my radio commentaries. Their book provides ample endnotes and documentation to buttress these conclusions.

Arthur Laffer, in a column in the *Wall Street Journal*, believes that "financial panics, if left alone, rarely cause much damage to the real economy."[67] But he then points out that government could not leave this financial meltdown alone. He laments that taxpayers have to pay for these bailouts because homeowners and lenders lost money. He notes: "If the house's value had appreciated, believe you me the overleveraged homeowners and the overly aggressive banks would never have shared their gain with the taxpayers."

He is also concerned with the ability of government to deal with the problem. He says, "Just watch how Congress and Barney Frank run the banks. If you thought they did a bad job running the post office, Amtrak, Fannie Mae, Freddie Mac and the military, just wait till you see what they'll do with Wall Street."

The reason the authors wrote *The End of Prosperity* was to set forth what has worked in the past as a prescription for the future. They were concerned that tax rates were headed up and not down, that the dollar is falling, and that America was turning it back on trade and globalization. They also were concerned that the federal budget was spiraling out of control and that various campaign promises (health care, energy policy,

---

[67] Arthur Laffer, "The Age of Prosperity Is Over," *Wall Street Journal*, 27 October, 2008, A19,online.wsj.com/article/SB122506830024970697.html.

environmental policy) would actually do more harm than good.

One of their final chapters is titled "The Death of Economic Sanity." They feared that the current push toward more governmental intervention would kill the economy. While they hoped that politicians would go slowly instead of launching an arsenal of economy killers, they weren't too optimistic. That is why they called their book *The End of Prosperity*.

The Future of Affluence

What do other economists have to say about our future? The Bible tells us that there is wisdom in many counselors (Proverbs 15:22). So when we see different economists essentially saying the same thing, we should pay attention.

Robert Samuelson, writing in *Newsweek* magazine, talks about "The Future of Affluence." He begins by talking about the major economic dislocations of the last few months:

Government has taken over mortgage giants Fannie Mae and Freddie Mac. The Treasury has made investments in many of the nation's major banks. The Federal Reserve is pumping out $1 trillion to stabilize credit markets. U.S. unemployment is at 6.1 percent, up from a recent low of 4.4 percent, and headed toward 8 percent, by some estimates.[68]

Samuelson says that a recovery will take place but we may find it unsatisfying. He believes we will lapse into a state of "affluent deprivation." By that he doesn't mean poverty, but he does mean that there will be a

---

[68] Robert Samuelson, "The Future of Affluence," Newsweek, 10 November 2008, 26-30.

state of mind in which people will feel poorer than they feel right now.

He says that the U.S. economy has benefited for roughly a quarter century "from the expansionary side effects of falling inflation—lower interest rates, greater debt, higher personal wealth—to the point now that we have now overdosed on its pleasures and are suffering a hangover." Essentially, prosperity bred habits, and many of these habits were bad habits. Personal savings went down, and debt and spending went up.

Essentially, we are suffering from "affluenza." Actually, that is the title of a book published many years ago to define the problem of materialism in general and consumerism in particular.

The authors say that the virus of affluenza "is not confined to the upper classes but has found it ways throughout our society. Its symptoms affect the poor as well as the rich . . . affluenza infects all of us, though in different ways."[69] The authors go on to say, "The affluenza epidemic is rooted in the obsessive, almost religious quest for economic expansion that has become the core principle of what is called the American dream."

Anyone looking at some of the social statistics for the U.S. might conclude that our priorities are out of whack. We spend more on shoes, jewelry, and watches than on higher education. We spend much more on auto maintenance than on religious and welfare activities. We have twice as many shopping centers as high schools.

The cure for the virus affluenza is a proper biblical perspective toward life. Jesus tells the parable of a rich man who decides to tear down his barns and build bigger ones (Luke 12:18) He is not satisfied with his current

---

[69] John DeGraaf, David Wann, and Thomas Naylor, Affluenza: The All-Consuming Epidemic, 2nd ed. (SF: Berrett-Koehler, 2005), xviii.

situation but is striving to make it better. Today most of us have adjusted to a life of affluence as normal and need to actively resist the virus of affluenza.

Squanderville

Another way to look at the economic future of America is to understand the story Warren Buffett tells of two side-by-side islands of equal size: Thriftville and Squanderville.[70]

On these islands, land is a capital asset. At first, the people on both islands are at a subsistence level and work eight hours a day to meet their needs. But the Thrifts realize that if they work harder and longer, they can produce a surplus of goods they can trade with the Squanders. Therefore, the Thrifts decide to do some serious saving and investing and begin to work sixteen hours a day. They begin exporting to Squanderville.

The people of Squanderville like the idea of working less. They can begin to live their lives free from toil. So they willingly trade for these goods with "Squanderbonds" that are denominated in "Squanderbucks."

Over time, the citizens of Thriftville accumulate lots of Squanderbonds. Some of the pundits in Squanderville see trouble. They foresee that the Squanders will now have to put in double time to eat and pay off their debt.

At about the same time, the citizens of Thriftville begin to get nervous and wonder if the Squanders will make good on their Squanderbonds (which are essentially IOUs). Therefore, the Thrifts start selling their Squanderbonds for Squanderbucks. Then they use the

---

[70] Warren Buffett, "America's Growing Trade Deficit Is Selling the Nation Out From Under Us," Fortune, 26 October 2003.

Squanderbucks to buy Squanderville land. Eventually, the Thrifts own all of Squanderville.

Now the citizens of Squanderville must pay rent to live on the land, which is owned by the Thrifts. The Squanders feel like they have been colonized by purchase rather than conquest. And they also face a horrible set of circumstances. They now must not only work eight hours in order to eat, but they must work additional hours to service the debt and pay Thriftville rent on the land they sold to them.

Does this story sound familiar? It should. Squanderville is America.

Economist Peter Schiff says that the United States has "been getting a free ride on the global gravy train." He sees other countries starting to reclaim their resources and manufactured goods. As a result, Americans are getting priced out of the market because these other countries are going to enjoy the consumption of goods that Americans previously purchased.

He says, "If America had maintained a viable economy and continued to produce goods instead of merely consuming them, and if we had saved money instead of borrowing, our standard of living could rise with everybody else's. Instead, we gutted our manufacturing, let our infrastructure decay, and encouraged our citizens to borrow with reckless abandon."[71]

It appears we have been infected with the virus of affluenza. The root problem is materialism that often breeds discontent. We want more of the world and its possessions rather than more of God and His will in our lives.

---

[71] Kirk Shinkle, "Permabear Peter Schiff's Worst-Case Scenario," U.S. News and World Report, 10 December 2008, tinyurl.com/63sqkh

What a contrast to what Paul says in Philippians where he counts all things to be loss (3:7-8) and instead has learned to be content (4:11). He goes on to talk about godliness with contentment in 1 Timothy 6:6-7. Contentment is an effective antidote to materialism and the foundation to a proper biblical perspective during these tough economic times.

CHAPTER 13 Consumerism and Materialism

Consumerism is a concern within society and within the church. So I would like to analyze both of these areas of concern by citing books that address this issue. The classic secular book on this subject is *Affluenza: The All-Consuming Epidemic*.[72] An excellent Christian book that deals with the topic of consumerism (in one of its chapters) is Michael Craven's book *Uncompromised Faith: Overcoming Our Culturalized Christianity*.[73]

Although many people use the terms consumerism and materialism interchangeable, there is a difference. Consumerism is much more than mere materialism. It is a way of perceiving the world that has affected all of us (especially Americans)—young and old, rich and poor, believer and non-believer—in significant ways. Essentially, it is a never-ending desire to possess material goods and to achieve personal success.

Others have defined consumerism as *having* rather than *being*.[74] Your worth and value are measured by what you have rather than by who you are. It is buying into a particular lifestyle in order to find your value, worth, and dignity. As Christians, we should be defined by the fact that we are created in God's image and have intrinsic worth and dignity.

---

[72] John DeGraaf, David Wann, and Thomas Naylor, Affluenza: The All-Consuming Epidemic, 2nd ed. (San Francisco: Berrett-Koehler, 2005).

[73] Michael Craven, Uncompromised Faith: Overcoming Our Culturalized Christianity (Colorado Springs, CO: NavPress, 2009).

[74] Richard John Neuhaus, Doing Well and Doing Good. The Challenge to the Christian Capitalist (New York: Doubleday, 1992), 52-53.

Most Americans do not have a biblical view of materialism and consumerism. A survey by George Barna found that 72 percent believe that God blesses people so they can enjoy life as much as possible. He also found that 81 percent believe the Bible teaches that God helps those who help themselves.[75]

Even secular writers see the problems with consumerism. The writers of *Affluenza* say that it is a virus that "is not confined to the upper classes but has found it way throughout our society. Its symptoms affect the poor as well as the rich . . . Affluenza infects all of us, though in different ways."[76]

The authors go on to say, "The *Affluenza* epidemic is rooted in the obsessive, almost religious quest for economic expansion that has become the core principle of what is called the American dream."[77]

Affluenza is rooted in a number of key concepts. First, it is rooted in the belief that the measure of national progress can be measured by the gross domestic product. Second, it is rooted in the idea that each generation must do better economically than the generation.

The consequences of this are devastating to both the nation and individuals. We are living in a time when the economic realities should be restraining spending (both as a nation and as individuals). Instead, we have corporately and individually pursued a lifestyle of "buy now and pay later" in order to expand economically. As we have discussed in previous articles, this philosophy has not served us well.

---

[75] George Barna, *The Second Coming of the Church* (Nashville, TN: Word, 1998), 21.

[76] Affluenza, xvii.

[77] Ibid., 3.

In an attempt to find happiness and contentment by pursuing "the good life," Americans have instead found it empty. Consumerism seems to promise fulfillment, but alas, it is merely an illusion. Consumerism does not satisfy.

Inverted Values and Changing Attitudes

Anyone looking at some of the social statistics for the U.S. might conclude that our priorities are out of whack. For example, we spend more on shoes, jewelry, and watches than on higher education. We spend much more on auto maintenance than on religious and welfare activities. And three times as many Americans buy Christmas presents for their pets than buy a present for their neighbors.[78]

Debt and waste also show skewed priorities. More Americans have declared personal bankruptcy than graduated from college. Our annual production of solid waste would fill a convoy of garbage trucks stretching halfway to the moon. We have twice as many shopping centers as high schools.[79] Americans seem to be working themselves to death in order to pay for everything they own or want to buy. We now work more hours each year than do the citizens of any other industrial country, including Japan. And according to Department of Labor statistics, full-time American workers are putting in one hundred sixty hours more (essentially one month more) than they did in 1969.[80] And ninety-five percent of our workers say the wish they could spend more time with their families.[81]

---

[78] U.S. Census Bureau, Statistical Abstract of the United States (Washington, DC: U.S. Government Printing Office, 2004-2005).

[79] Affluenza, 4.

[80] Ibid., 42.

[81] Ibid., 4.

111

Americans do recognize the problem and are trying to simplify their lives. A poll by the Center for a New American Dream showed a change in attitudes and action. The poll revealed that eighty-five percent of Americans think our priorities are out of whack. For example, nearly nine in ten (eighty-eight percent) said American society is too materialistic. They also found that most Americans (ninety-three percent) feel we are too focused on working and making money. They also believed (ninety-one percent) that we buy and consume more than we need. More than half of Americans (fifty-two percent) said they have too much debt.[82]

The poll found that many Americans were taking steps to work less, even if that meant reducing their consuming. Nearly half of Americans (forty-eight percent) say they voluntarily made changes in their life in order to get more time and have a less stressful life. This increase in the number of self-proclaimed "down-shifters" suggests the beginning of a national change in priorities.

Perhaps Americans are coming to the realization that more consumer goods do not make them happy. Think back to the year 1957. That was the year that the program *Leave it to Beaver* premiered on television. It was also the year that the Russians shot Sputnik into space. That was a long time ago.

However, 1957 is significant for another reason. It was that year that Americans described themselves as "very happy" reached a plateau.[83] Since then there has been an ever declining percentage of Americans who describe themselves that way even though the size of the average home today is twice what it was in the 1950s

---

[82] Center for a New American Dream, 2004 survey, www.newdream.org/about/pdfs/PollRelease.pdf.

[83] David Myers, The American Paradox (New Haven, CT: Yale University Press, 2000), 136.

and these homes are filled with consumer electronics someone back then could only dream about.

Undermining the Family and Church

What has been the impact of consumerism? Michael Craven talks about how consumerism has undermined the family and the church.

The family has been adversely affected by the time pressures created by a consumer mentality. Family time used to be insulated to a degree from employment demands. That is no longer true. "We no longer hesitate to work weekends and evenings or to travel Sundays, for example, in order to make the Monday-morning meeting."[84] As we have already mentioned, Americans are working more hours than ever before. The signal that is being sent throughout the corporate world is that you must be willing to sacrifice time with your family in order to get ahead. And that is exactly what is taking place.

Sociologists have concluded, "Since 1969 the time American parents spend with their children has declined by 22 hours per week."[85] Some have questioned this study because its estimate of the decline came from subtracting increased employment hours of parents from total waking hours. However, I believe it makes the point that families are suffering from consumerism, and this study parallels other studies that have looked at the decline in quality parent-child interaction at home.

The bottom line is this: Americans may talk about family values and quality time with their kids, but their behavior demonstrates that they don't live those values.

---

[84] Craven, Uncompromised Faith, 79.

[85] L.C. Sayer, et. All, "Are Parents Investing Less in Children," paper presented at the American Sociological Association annual meeting, August 2000.

113

Frequently children and their needs are sacrificed on the altar of career success. The marketplace trumps family time more than we would like to think that it does.

The church has also been undermined by consumerism. Busy lifestyles and time pressures crowd out church attendance. Weekly church attendance has reached an all-time low in America. And even for those who try to attend church regularly, attendance is sometimes hit-or-miss. Years ago I realized how difficult it was to teach a series in a Sunday School class because there was so little continuity in attendance from one week to the next.

Craven points out that those who are dissatisfied with a consumerist-created lifestyle turn to church for meaning and purpose. Unfortunately, they think that: "by integrating a 'little religion' into their lives, they will balance and perfect the lifestyle. Tragically, they do not realize it is not their lifestyle that is in need of salvation; it is their very souls."[86]

Consumerism also affects the way we go about the Christian life. Religious consumerists add spiritual disciplines to their life in the same way they approach work (as a task to be fulfilled with measurable goals). In the end, spiritual activity becomes one more item on a to-do list.

Craven reminds us that Jesus Christ is not to be treated as one good among many. Jesus Christ should be the supreme Good and the source of all life.

---

[86] Affluenza, 80.

Undermining the Community and Character

What has been the impact of consumerism? Craven talks about how consumerism has undermined community and how it has also undermined virtue and character. "With the increased priority given to the marketplace, there follows a decreased commitment to neighbors, community, and connections to extended family; children are displaced in pursuit of opportunities, and familial priorities become subverted to company demands."[87]

This has an adverse impact on citizenship. People are no longer citizens but consumers. Citizens have duties and responsibilities to their fellow citizens. Consumers do not. They are merely partaking of what the consumer economy provides for them. Citizens care about others and their community. Consumers only care about what the society can provide to them.

Christian philosopher Francis Schaeffer predicted that as society moved from the "death of God" to what today we can call the "death of truth" there would only be two things left: "personal peace and personal prosperity." Schaeffer argued that once Americans accepted these values, they would sacrifice everything to protect their personal peace and affluence.[88]

Consumerism also undermines virtue and character. It "shifts the objective of human life away from cultivating virtue and character, knowing truth, and being content to an artificially constructed, idealized lifestyle

---

[87] Ibid.

[88] Francis Schaeffer, How Should We Then Live? (Old Tappan: NJ: Fleming Revell, 1976), 205.

115

that is continually reinforced through media, entertainment, and advertising."[89]

With this view of life, things become more important than people. Having is more important than being. And it is a lifestyle that pursues distraction (sports, entertainment, hobbies, etc.) almost in an effort to keep from thinking about the real world and its circumstances.

As we have already noted, consumerism does not satisfy. In fact, it can be argued that a consumerist mentality puts us in an emotional place where we are perpetually discontent. We are unable to rest in that which is good because we always want more. This is made even more difficult in our world where advertising images provide a seemingly endless series of choices that are promoted to us as necessary in order to achieve the perfect life.

Michael Craven points out that when Christians talk about being content; this is often ridiculed as being willing to "settle for less" and even condemned as "lazy, defeatist, and even irresponsible."[90] Instead, we are spurred on by talk of "doing all things to the glory of God" which can be used to justify a consumerist mentality.

A Biblical Perspective on Materialism and Consumerism

We live in a culture that encourages us to buy more and more. No longer are we encouraged to live within our means. We are tempted to buy more than just the necessities and tempted to spend more on luxuries. The Bible warns us about this. Proverbs 21:17 says, "He who loves pleasure will become a poor man; He who loves wine and oil will not become rich."

---

[89] Affluenza, 81.
[90] Ibid., 83.

In our lifetimes, we have lots of money that flows through our hands, and we need to make wiser choices. Consider that a person who makes just $25,000 a year will in his lifetime have a million dollars pass through his hands. The median family income in America is twice that. That means that two million dollars will pass through the average American family's hands.

A tragic aspect of consumerism is that there is never enough. There is always the desire for more because each purchase only satisfies for short while. Then there is the need for more and more. Essentially, it is the law of diminishing returns. Economists use a more technical term—the law of diminishing marginal return. Simply put, the more we get, the less it satisfies and the more we want.

Once again, the Bible warns us about this. Haggai 1:5-6 says, "Now therefore, thus says the Lord of hosts, 'Consider your ways! You have sown much, but harvest little; you eat, but there is not enough to be satisfied; you drink, but there is not enough to become drunk; you put on clothing, but no one is warm enough; and he who earns, earns wages to put into a purse with holes.'"

We should also be responsible citizens. A tragic consequence of consumerism is what it does to the average citizen. James Kunstler, author of *The Geography of Nowhere*, believes we have "mutated from citizens to consumers." He says, "Consumers have no duties or responsibilities or obligations to their fellow consumers. Citizens do. They have the obligation to care about their fellow citizens and about the integrity of the town's environment and history."[91]

America was once a nation of joiners. Alexis de Tocqueville noted this in his book *Democracy in America*.

---

[91] James Kunstler in discussion with David Wann, March 1997, quoted in Affluenza, 65.

Americans would join in all sorts of voluntary associations. However, we seem to no longer be joiners but loners. Sure, there are still many people volunteering and giving their time. However, much of this is "on the run" as we shuffle from place to place in our busy lives.

Christians are called to be the salt of the earth (Matthew 5:13) and the light of the world (Matthew 5:14-16). We are also called to be ambassadors for Christ (2 Corinthians 5:20). We must resist the temptations of consumerism that encourage us to focus on ourselves and withdraw from active involvement in society.

APPENDIX Bible Verses on Economics and Finance

1. Planning and budgeting

Proverbs 6:6-8; Proverbs 13:16; Proverbs 14:15; Proverbs 21:5; Proverbs 22:3; Proverbs 27:1; Luke 14:28-30; Ephesians 5:15-16

2. Learning contentment

Ecclesiastes 5:10; Matthew 6:25-26; Luke 12:15; Philippians 4:11-13; 1 Timothy 6:6-8; Hebrews 13:5

3. Avoiding greed and materialism

Proverbs 28:20-22; Luke 12:15; 1 Corinthians 7:31; 1 Timothy 6:9-10

4. Avoiding debt

Psalm 37:21; Proverbs 2:7; Proverbs 22:7; Romans 13:8; 1 Timothy 5:8

5. Giving and tithing

Proverbs 3:9-10; Malachi 3:8-10; Matthew 6:1-4; Luke 6:38; 1 Corinthians 16:1-2; 2 Corinthians 8:2-3; 2 Corinthians 9:6-9

6. Investing

Proverbs 10:4; Proverbs 13:11; Proverbs 15:22; Proverbs 21:20; Ecclesiastes 11:2

Bibliography

Anderson, Kerby. *Making the Most of Your Money in Tough Times.* Eugene, OR: Harvest House, 2009.

Craven, Michael. *Uncompromised Faith: Overcoming Our Culturalized Christianity.* Colorado Springs, CO: NavPress, 2009.

DeGraaf, John, David Wann, and Thomas Naylor. *Affluenza: The All-Consuming Epidemic.* San Francisco: Berrett-Koehler, 2005.

Fishman, Charles. *The Wal-Mart Effect.* New York: Penguin, 2006.

Friedman, Thomas. *The World is Flat: A Brief History of the Twentieth Century.* New York: Farrar, Straus and Giroux, 2005.

Hayek, F.A. *The Road to Serfdom: Text and Documents, the Definitive Edition ed. Bruce Caldwell.* Chicago: University of Chicago Press, 2007.

Laffer, Arthur, Stephen Moore, and Peter Tanous. *The End of Prosperity.* New York: Simon and Schuster, 2008.

Richards, Jay. *Money, Greed, and God.* New York: Harper One, 2009.

Smith, Adam. *The Wealth of Nations.* 1776.

Stapleford, John. *Bulls, Bears & Golden Calves.* Downers Grove, IL: Intervsrsity Pres, 2002.

Other Books by Kerby Anderson

CHRISTIAN PUBLISHING HOUSE & PROBE MINISTRIES

CHRISTIANS AND GOVERNMENT
A Biblical Point of View

KERBY ANDERSON

CHRISTIANS AND GOVERNMENT: A Biblical Point of View by Kerby Anderson

$5.95

If Our Books are Not What the Book Description Claims—100% Money Back If Bought Here!

Print List Price: $9.95

CPH Price: $5.95

Save $4.00 (40%)

Product Details

Paperback: 142 pages

Publisher: Christian Publishing House (July 12, 2016)

Language: English

ISBN-13: 978-1-945757-00-6

ISBN-10: 1-945757-00-0

Product Dimensions: 5" x 8"

Also in eBook Format

Kindle eBook Amazon: $4.95

Nook eBook Barnes & Noble: $4.95

Kobo eBooks: $4.95

Google eBooks: $4.95

Book Description

Government affects our daily lives, and Christians need to think about how to apply biblical principles to politics and government. This book provides an overview of the biblical principles relating to what the apostle Paul calls "governing authorities" (i.e., government) with specific chapters dealing with the founding principles of the American government. This includes an examination of the Declaration of Independence, the Constitution, the Bill of Rights, and the Federalist Papers.

The thirteen chapters in this book not only look at the broad founding principles but also provide an in-depth look at other important political and governmental issues. One section explains the history and application of church and state issues. Another section describes aspects of political debate and discourse. A final section provides a brief overview of the Christian heritage of this nation that was important in the founding of this country and the framing of our founding documents.

Some questions that Anderson will answer are: Is it possible for humans to establish a government that will actually bring lasting peace and security? What are some of the important biblical principles in establishing government? What hinders human efforts in setting up and maintaining the perfect government? How can we develop discernment and make wise choices about candidates and governmental policies? What is the answer to the problems of corruption and oppression? Why should we seriously consider what the Bible says about what the apostle Paul called "governing authorities" and our future?

Author Biography

KERBY ANDERSON is the President of Probe Ministries. He also serves as a visiting professor at Dallas Theological Seminary and has spoken on dozens of university campuses including University of Michigan, Vanderbilt University, Princeton University, Johns Hopkins University, University of Colorado and University of Texas. He is the host of "Point of View" radio talk show and regular guest on "Fire Away" (American Family Radio). He has appeared or numerous radio and TV talk shows including the "MacNeil/Lehrer News Hour," "Focus on the Family," "Beverly LaHaye Live," and "The 700 Club." He is the author of thirteen books.

B.S., Oregon State University (Zoology)

M.F.S., Yale University (Science)

M.A., Georgetown University (Government)

Kennedy Institute of Bioethics (Washington, D.C)

Made in the USA
San Bernardino, CA
07 September 2018